The Bedside, Bathtub & Armchair Companion to Dickens

The Bedside, Bathtub & Armchair Companion to

Dickens

Brian Murray

CONTINUUM • LONDON • NEW YORK

2009

The Continuum International Publishing Group Inc.
80 Maiden Lane, New York, NY 10038

The Continuum International Publishing Group Ltd
The Tower Building, 11 York Road, London SE1 7NX

www.continuumbooks.com

Printed in the United States of America

9780826418821

The publisher has applied for CIP data.

Contents

"How often one really thinks about any writer, even a writer one cares for, is a difficult thing to decide; but I should doubt whether anyone who has actually read Dickens can go a week without remembering him in one context or another. Whether you approve of or not, he is there, like the Nelson Column. At any moment some scene or character, which may come from some book you cannot even remember the name of, is liable to drop into your mind. Micawber's letters! Winkle in the witness-box! Mrs. Gamp! Mrs. Wititterly and Sir Tumley Snuffin! Todger's! Mrs. Leo Hunter! Squeers! Silas Wegg and the Decline and Fall-off of the Russian Empire! Miss Mills and the Desert of Sahara! Wopsle acting Hamlet! Mrs. Jellyby! Mantalini, Jerry Cruncher, Barkis, Pumblechook, Tracy Tupman, Skimpole, Joe Gargery, Pecksniff—and so it goes on and on. It is not so much a series of books, it is more like a world."

— George Orwell,
"Charles Dickens," 1939

CHARLES DICKENS

Inimitable

....

fter more than a decade of literary fame, Charles Dickens started to think about writing an autobiography. It wasn't a chore he welcomed, but he was increasingly the subject of sometimes "wildly imaginative" stories appearing in the British and American press. In 1842, after reading one of these accounts, Dickens jokingly swore that he might "one of these days be induced to lay violent hands upon myself—in other words attempt my own life."

Dickens (1812-1870) was a phenomenon, and his story was unprecedented in many ways. After he achieved early success, his influence grew, and he became—in a very modern way—a celebrity, the most recognized writer of his day. Dickens' novels were international bestsellers; his characters too Mr. Pickwick, Sam Weller, Oliver Twist—became household names. Dickens was himself "wildly imaginative" and a widely respected public figure actively engaged with a wide range of social issues and debates.

Dickens was on permanent display for most of his life. He relished his success and the many benefits of fame. But he was also private and not proud of every aspect of his character or his life's story. So it's not surprising that Charles Dickens never did write *The Life of Charles Dickens*. He left the job and the title to John Forster, whose three-volume biography first appeared just two years after the great writer's death.

Forster dreaded the task. He knew Dickens too well, he believed, having been his closest friend for many years. In the end Forster was discreet, as Dickens assumed he would be. He was admiring too. But he wasn't worshipful, and the Dickens Forster presents is, in all essentials, the thoroughly examined Dickens biographers describe today. He is estimable and exasperating, brilliantly funny and often very angry: high-minded, petty, markedly generous, fiercely productive, and intensely self-absorbed.

In fact, Forster's biography stunned many readers and critics who were struck not only by the ferocity with which Dickens managed his career, but by the revelation that the hearty author of *The Pickwick Papers* and *A Christmas Carol* had been so often discontented and haunted by events from his boyhood years. Dickens' childhood, as Forster related, was a tale of innocence and experience, of light and dark—of being cast from a garden of security and indulgence into a world of struggle and neglect.

Dickens belonged by birth to what might be called the aspiring servant class. To be sure his mother, Elizabeth Barrow, had grown up secure and fairly well-schooled in a comfortable middle-class milieu, the daughter of a senior administrator in the pay office of the Royal Navy. But Dickens' grandparents, on his father's side, worked—as steward and housekeeper—for John Crewe, later Lord Crewe, a member of Parliament and an influential Whig. Dickens' grandfather died in 1785, the same year that John Dickens, the novelist's father, was born. But for many years Dickens' grandmother remained on Lord Crewe's household staff, attending diligently to her duties, and—as one Dickens biography put it—rearing her children "as genteel copies of the upstairs people."

With Crewe's help, John Dickens became at nineteen a pay clerk in the navy Pay Office in London, where he met the Barrows, and showed every indication of moving duly up the ranks. After a two-year courtship, John and Elizabeth were married and moved first to Portsmouth, where, in 1810, their first child, Fanny, was born. Charles was next. Over the next thirteen years six more children followed, but two, a boy and a girl, died in infancy.

When Dickens was five, his family moved to Chatham, near Rochester, in Kent—a place he remembered fondly. For about four years the young Dickens family lived well in a roomy house,

Dickens

employing a nanny and a maid. John called himself a gentleman, hosted parties, and donated funds to local charities. He boosted his children's talents. Fanny, he noted, was musical, and Charles had a charming gift for singing comical songs. John, proud of the boy, stood him on tabletops and let him perform to the applause of neighbors and friends.

Charles was slight for his age and often sickly; "he was never a first-rate hand at marbles," Forster admits, "or peg-top, or prisoner's base." But he was clever—"a boy of capacity," in the words of William Giles, the Chatham schoolmaster who first took note of his precocious skills. By the time he was ten or eleven, Dickens had read most of the books in his father's library, including *Tom Jones, Roderick Random, Peregrine Pickle, Humphrey Clinker, The Vicar of Wakefield, Robinson Crusoe,* and— a particular favorite—*The Arabian Nights.* These and other popular titles "kept alive my fancy," Dickens writes in the autobiographical *David Copperfield*:

> I have been Tom Jones (a child's Tom Jones, a harmless creature) for a week together. I have sustained my own idea of Roderick Random for a month at a stretch, I verily believe. I had a greedy relish for a few volumes of voyages and travels— I forgot what, now—that were on those shelves; and for days and days I can remember to have gone about my region of our house, armed with the centre-piece out of an old set of boot-trees: the perfect realization of Captain Somebody, of the Royal Navy, in danger of being beset by savages....When I think of it, the picture always rises in my mind, of a summer evening, boys at play in the churchyard, and I sitting on my bed reading as if for life.

But John and Elizabeth Dickens, sociable and well-intentioned, could not make their household run. Elizabeth, at least in Dickens' characterization, was impulsive and flighty. John liked his drink. He was very good at borrowing money and very bad at paying it back. In 1822, when John Dickens was transferred back to London, he probably believed—wrongly, it turned out—that he was outrunning his creditors and all set for another fresh start.

For several decades Dickens did not discuss the complications of his childhood years. Even Forster was surprised to learn that, not long after he resettled his family in London, John Dickens was back in financial crisis and evading the law; that he was finally arrested and carted off to the Marshalsea, a debtor's jail. Before then, in an effort to stay afloat, his family had pawned books and furniture and Mrs. Dickens managed somehow to start a school, posting a sign—"Mrs. Dickens's Establishment"—and sending Charles off with handbills to announce its debut. But "nobody ever came to the school," Dickens told Forster. "Nor do I recollect that anybody ever proposed to come, or that the least preparation was made to receive anybody."

The Flower-Girl

For Charles, however, more trauma loomed. One of his mother's relatives had found him work in a blacking factory next to the Thames, near Hungerford Stairs. Charles was hired to affix labels to jars of Warren's boot polish, sold throughout the British Isles. Business was good for Warren's, but its products, as Dickens told Forster, were made in a "crazy, tumble-down" warehouse where, as he worked, he could hear rats, "swarming down in the cellars, and the sound of their squeaking and scuffling coming up the stairs at all times."

Thus had the wheel of fortune turned. Through no fault of his own, the star pupil of his little local school—a boy who could conjugate Latin verbs and had already written a play, *Misnar, the Sultan of India*—was now stuck in a rat-filled warehouse, put to toil beside poor, unschooled boys with no expectations of their own. It was all so bewildering and unfair. Somehow, Charles' sister Fanny had been allowed to keep up her studies at the Royal Academy of Music. And his younger siblings had joined their parents in family quarters at the Marshalsea, an accepted practice at the time. But there was poor Charles, quite on his own, lodged in a rented room some distance away.

And so one pictures him walking to and from Warren's at dawn and dusk, passing among beggars, pickpockets, flower girls, and crossing-sweepers—the sort of weary urban strugglers one finds in Henry Mayhew's portrait of *London Labour London Poor* (1851). At Warren's, bustling about for long hours with his paste pots and scissors, Charles was teased by young workmates who found it quite droll to find this "young gentleman" dropped into their midst.

John Dickens was, as Forster revealed, the main model for Wilkins Micawber in *David Copperfield*, Dickens' most directly autobiographical novel. He was a man of stark moods and was often low. But imprisonment, he found, wasn't that bad. The pseudo-aristocratic manner he cultivated ("airy," "chatty," "a little pompous," as some acquaintances described it) set him apart from the other inmates and compensated for his threadbare state. He was popular at the Marshalsea as a source of diversion and avuncular advice. Mr. Dickens may have been housing his family behind a prison wall, but he was also free for the time from financial pressures, and every day he held center stage.

Charles also enjoyed his father's performances. Once, visiting the Marshalsea, he watched quietly as a long line of men entered his family's cramped room to sign a petition to the Queen composed, with typical floridness, by John Dickens himself. One "Captain Porter (who had washed himself, to do honour to so solemn an occasion)" read out the petition "in a loud, sonorous voice," as Dickens told Forster. "I remember a certain luscious roll he gave to such words as 'Majesty—gracious Majesty—your Gracious Majesty's unfortunate subjects—your Majesty's well-known munificence'—as if the words were something real in his mouth, and delicious to taste: my poor father meanwhile listening with a little of an author's vanity, and contemplating (not severely) the spikes on the opposite wall."

"Whatever was comical in this scene," Dickens told Forster, "and whatever was pathetic, I sincerely believe I perceived in my corner, whether I demonstrated or not, quite as well as I should perceive it now. I made out my own little character and story for every man who put his name to the sheet of paper." Their "different peculiarities of dress, of face, of gait, of manner, were written indelibly upon my memory. I would rather have seen it than the best play ever played."

A Turn of Events

And then, as if in a play, a small pension arrived and a modest inheritance, and suddenly John Dickens was out of the Marshalsea. Charles understandably assumed that he too would be released from the warehouse—but his mother had other plans. His small wage, she calculated, was still vital to the household fund. Charles, she insisted, must stick to his post. Dickens told Forster that he never quite forgave his parents and particularly his mother for treating him not like a boy of capacity, but a little wage slave. From the start, he told Forster, they both seemed "quite satisfied" with his career in the blacking factory: "they could hardly have been more so, if I had been twenty years of age, distinguished at a grammar school, and going to Cambridge."

Warren's had moved to a new building, and now placed its young workers beside a street-level window where in a strong light their brisk industry could be admired by passers-by. And so young Charles Dickens, once cheered for his songs and comical stories, was now drawing attention as a harried drudge. Finally, his pride struck, John Dickens stopped his son's laboring and put him in school.

It was not a very good school. The Wellington House Academy, despite certain pretensions, mainly prepared lower-middle-class boys for modest careers as clerks. Dickens mocked the place and its eccentric faculty in an 1851 essay, "Our School." The Latin master was "a colourless doubled-up near-sighted man with a crutch, who was always cold, and always putting onions into his ears for deafness, and ... always applying a ball of pocket-handkerchief to some part of his face with a screwing action round and round." And William Jones, the headmaster, was a vulgar bully: "The only branches of education with which he showed the least acquaintance, were, ruling and corporally punishing. He was always ruling ciphering-books with a bloated mahogany ruler, smiting the palms of offenders with the same diabolical instrument, or viciously drawing a pair of pantaloons tight with one of his large hands and caning the wearer with the other."

Clearly the events of Dickens' early years, so closely associated with feelings of abandonment and shame, left a lingering wound. Dickens himself told Forster that, even as an adult, he could not bear to go near the old Warren's warehouse, for "a certain smell of the cement they put upon the blacking corks" always brought grim memories "of what I was once." Passing the place "made me cry," Dickens admitted, even "after my eldest child could speak."

And yet, these events, he said, "have worked together to make me what I am." Early on, he found energy in adversity. Early on, he lost confidence in his parents and, for better or worse, seized full control of his life through the relentless application of his will. Dickens may have inherited, from his father, both a love of language and a theatrical flair. But he was determined to succeed where his father had failed.

Certainly, at the Wellington House Academy, Dickens applied himself eagerly and left his mark. Other former students did not recall a morose or cringing boy, but one "full of animation and animal spirits" who "probably was connected with every mischievous prank at the school." Charles formed a story-writing club and staged plays; he won prizes; he invented "a sort of lingo," another schoolmate recalled, "which made us quite unintelligible to bystanders." Another pictured Dickens

> Leading us in Drummond Street in pretending to be poor boys and asking the passers-by for charity—especially old ladies, one of whom told us she 'had no money for beggar boys.' On these adventures, when the old ladies were quite staggered by the impudence of the demand, Dickens would explode with laughter and take to his heels.

Nothing in Dickens' background—not least his family's indigence—encouraged him to think of actually going to Cambridge, or any other university. And so, like most young men of his time and class, he set out at fifteen to face the world. He began as a clerk in the law office of Ellis and Blackmore in Holborn Court. Dickens found the work—bookkeeping, copying documents—dull beyond belief. But he liked the other office-lads and often joined them for an evening of mirth in theatres or pubs. London offered plenty of cabarets, music-halls, and conjuring shows where young men-about-town might disport themselves; there were also "private" theatres where, for a fee, an amateur actor could put on a costume and play out a couple of scenes as, say, Richard III. Dickens was already deeply drawn to London's dramatic venues, and by the time he was twenty he went to theatres almost every night.

At the same time Dickens often visited the library at the British Museum, hoping a regimen of self-schooling might balance out somewhat his patchy education and lack of a university degree. He also taught himself shorthand, useful in several careers. Trained in a complex system of lines, squiggles, and dots, a skilled shorthand writer was like a human tape recorder, able to render a speech or debate with precise accuracy. But mastering the method was not easy, as Dickens stressed, "being about equal in difficulty to the mastery of six languages." (David Copperfield, another shorthand adept, recalled the challenge of mastering the system this way: "the changes that were rung upon dots, which in such a position meant such a thing, and in such a position something else entirely different; the wonderful vagaries that were played by circles; the unaccountable consequences that resulted from marks like flies' legs; the tremendous effects of a curve in a wrong place, not only troubled my waking hours, but reappeared before me in my sleep.") Dickens, though, quickly learned the system, and was soon dazzling his colleagues and friends with the sharpness of his ear and the swiftness of his hand. Years later Dickens would still describe himself, perhaps only half-jokingly, as "the best shorthand writer in the world."

**"The Cock" Tavern
Fleet Street**

Tiring of the law, Dickens began covering the House of Commons as a shorthand reporter in 1831. He was employed by the *Mirror of Parliament*, a new weekly that, like *Hansard*, looked to provide an accurate record of governmental proceedings and debates. The *Mirror of Parliament* was owned by one of his mother's brothers, John Barrow, who—as it turned out—played a crucial role in boosting Dickens' young career. Charles enjoyed the work, and the pressure of deadlines, and all the camaraderie, intrigue and rivalry that came with a life in the press. He would always love newspapers in all of their various glories. Many years later, Dickens addressed a meeting of news vendors and praised them for dispensing all those "wonderful broadsheets" that were, he believed, "indispensible to civilization and freedom."

In 1830 Dickens had met Maria Beadnell, the daughter of a London banker. Dickens courted her intently, incessantly, and in vain. Understandably, his biographers have made much of the episode, for this obsession with "the Pocket Venus" (as Maria's friends called her) had, as Dickens told Forster, "excluded every other idea from my mind for years, at a time of life when four years are equal to four times four." He was shattered when, in 1833, Maria, presumably pressured by her parents, told Dickens he should please stop coming round. "I have never loved," Dickens told her, "and I could never love any human creature breathing but yourself."

A Dynamic Age

The Beadnell episode, as Dickens told Forster, exposed the "desperate intensity of my nature." It also seems to have sparked further his great drive to succeed. By 1834, Dickens was doing less transcribing and more actual reporting for the *Morning Chronicle*, a liberal daily with a long record of distinguished contributors, including, before Dickens, William Hazlitt and Samuel Coleridge. The young Dickens covered political events and elections in British cities and towns at a time of robust political debate: during the 1830s, Parliament passed the Reform Bill (which began a gradual expansion of voting rights) and debated the Factory Act (which regulated child labour), the Emancipation Act (which freed slaves in British colonies), and the Poor Law Amendment Act (which put in place a national board of commissioners to oversee the administration of poor relief). He quite enjoyed the thrill of racing back to London after covering some meeting or speech and "writing on the palm of my hand, by the light of a dark lantern, in a post-chaise and four, galloping through a wild country, and through the dead of the night, at the then surprising rate of fifteen miles an hour." At one rally it rained so hard that, as Dickens fondly recalled, two friendly colleagues "held a pocket-handkerchief over my note-book, after the manner of a state canopy in an ecclesiastical procession."

Temple Bar, London

Queen Victoria's long reign—from 1837 to 1901—was of course marked by far-reaching scientific and technological discoveries, and by the global amplification of British power; by the growth of cities, a rise in literacy, and a great adjustment of the social order as wealth and poverty grew, and more and more people aspired to and achieved their place in the expanding middle class. Thus the Victorian Dickens is recognizably modern too—an acute observer of the opportunities and complications that beset people living in dynamic economies during rapidly changing times.

But Dickens was an imaginative writer and a journalist, not a politician or a political theorist; and while he famously backed many progressive causes (including the expansion of education, the improvement of schools, and the wide institution of measures meant to protect industrial workers), he was not a consistent spokesman for any particular party or economic theory. His favorite political commentator—if that's the right term—was the great, idiosyncratic Thomas Carlyle, whose diverse writings, largely neglected today, comprise a long and artful fulmination against utilitarianism, materialism, and greed. "We plead and speak, in our Parliaments and elsewhere," Carlyle once characteristically complained, "not as from the Soul, but from the Stomach;—wherefore, indeed, our pleadings are so slow to profit."

Dickens did sometimes refer to himself as a "radical" and later a "liberal," terms that now carry rather different connotations than they did in Dickens' day. For Dickens, broadly and essentially, liberalism indicated middle class entrepreneurism— free trade not primarily controlled by the interests of old, amply privileged aristocratic families. It also implied a generalized belief in "progress" that embraced not only the wider advancement of science and education, but the support of reasonable measures to both aid and uplift the poor. But such progress wasn't solely or even largely contingent on the efforts of government; as his works repeatedly show, Dickens believed, perhaps quixotically and apparently with less optimism as the years went by, that wide social changes and improvements would arrive when many more people became less selfish, and more true to the virtues of mercy and charity proclaimed by their own Christian faith.

In fact, Dickens' own experience as a parliamentary reporter left him "with small respect for our House of Commons," as he once phrased it with ironic understatement. From the start he was struck by his perception that so many of Britain's ruling elite were such mediocre men, complacent toffs or blustering tycoons, who could not see an inch beyond their own selfish concerns. At the height of his influence Dickens continued to suggest that Britain's most powerful leaders were still, in effect, blundering about in the Feudal Age, blind to the challenges that would surely intensify in the years ahead. The country would be better run, he complained in an 1855 essay, by "any half-dozen shopkeepers taken at random from the London Directory and shot into Downing Street out of sacks." Still, no matter how bitterly he attacked "rabid Tories" or how frequently he called parliament the "national dust yard" or similar names, Dickens never quite backed away from the ideal of rational representative government: he was too aware of the dangers of the mob and the dangers of the dictator to align himself with anything else. He was after reform, not revolution.

During these years of covering politics and courting Maria Beadnell, Dickens also pursued his dramatic interests: he sang at recitals, acted in amateur productions, and closely studied the techniques of top performers like Charles Mathews, a singer and ventriloquist famous for the range and accuracy of his imitations. Mathews could do the Police in different voices—as well as Scotsmen, Frenchmen, Italians, and other overdrawn ethnic types. He'd stage scenes in which these comical characters would converse, distinguished not only by their accents, but other tag-lines or quirks of speech. Dickens followed the example in *The Pickwick Papers,* among other places, where Mr. Jingle with his staccato syntax enlivens the action; and in *David Copperfield,* where Uriah Heep repeatedly insists that he is a very "umble man."

"Novelty, pleasant to most people, is particularly delightful, I think, to me."

Dickens always believed he could prospered as a professional stage entertainer, and many of his friends—including Thomas Carlyle and his wife, Jane, tough critics both—agreed. "Dickens' essential faculty," wrote Carlyle, "is that of a first-rate Playactor; had he been born twenty of forty years sooner, we should most probably have had a second and greater Mathews ... and no writing Dickens." But writing, Dickens saw, paid. All over London the demand for fresh copy was high. And in 1833 Dickens, who had been writing stories and sketches since childhood, sent his first humorous story, "A Dinner at Poplar Walk," to the small *Monthly Magazine.*

Boz is Born

It's a funny piece, centering upon the sort of put-upon misanthrope that the vaudevillian W.C. Fields, a great Dickens fan, made famous in the movies a century later. "There were two classes of created objects," Dickens relates, that Mr. Augustus Minns "held in the deepest and utmost unmingled horror; these were dogs and children." Mr. Minns soon comes face-to-face with "a large white dog, dressed in a suit of fleecy hosiery," and—at the dinner he is loath to attend—with an energetic eight-year-old boy who promptly pokes at Minns with his mama's parasol. Minns "was not unamiable, but he could, at any time, have viewed the execution of a dog, or the assassination of an infant, with the liveliest satisfaction."

The success of "Dinner" (it was promptly pirated) encouraged the young writer to turn out other sketches of a similar kind. Many of these first appeared, to wide notice, in the morning and evening editions of the *Chronicle* under the byline "Boz"—once the family nickname for Dickens' younger brother, Augustus.

The journalist and novelist Harrison Ainsworth, whose career was also taking off, now made a point of bringing Dickens more fully into London's literary scene. Dickens met editors and publishers eager to have his work, including John Macrone, who in 1836 published *Sketches By Boz* with illustrations by George Cruikshank, a leading caricaturist and part of the outer ring of Dickens' circle for several years to come.

Sketches By Boz offered a fresh blend of satire, sentiment, and sharp observation that proved profitable to Macrone and Dickens alike. But it was the *Pickwick Papers*, which also first appeared in 1836, that put Dickens so decidedly in a class by himself. *Pickwick* began as a serial project for Robert Seymour, another popular illustrator who had come up with a series of drawings of eccentric "sportsmen" comically engaged in outdoor pursuits. Initially, Dickens was hired to supply text for Seymour's illustrations. But Boz took charge, insisting that Seymour's pictures must support the words. Reluctantly, Seymour and the serial's publishers, Chapman and Hall, agreed. *Pickwick* appeared in monthly installment, but first sales proved slow. And then in April 1836, Seymour, a chronic depressive, committed suicide.

(top)Young Dickens; and Harrison Ainsworth

Dickens soon found a replacement, Hablot Knight Browne, a shy young artist who, unlike Seymour, quickly grasped that the key to working productively with Dickens was to let Dickens call the shots. Browne soon named himself "Phiz," to better chime with Boz, who in turn soon found the ingredients to give *Pickwick* its distinctive and popular flavor. He'd already come up with some strong comic portraits for the novel, including—besides Jingle— the drowsy Fat Boy and Samuel Pickwick himself, the cheery bachelor who sets out to get the measure of the world in all of its grand mysterious forms. But Dickens' hero was perhaps rather too plump and sunny; he needed someone sharp nearby: he needed shade.

And so, in Chapter Ten, Dickens added Sam Weller to serve as Pickwick's valet and to provide (with his father, Tony, a coach driver) much of the serial's most inspired verbal comedy. Even now readers are likely to view him, with John Forster, as "one of those people that take their place among the supreme successes of fiction, as one that nobody ever saw but everybody recognizes, at once perfectly natural and intensely original." As sketched by Phiz, Weller wore his hat at a jaunty angle and conveyed a shrewd, streetwise air. Sales soared.

Dickens agreed to do *Pickwick* partly out of a pressing per-sonal financial need: he was about to be married. In 1834 he had met his fiancée, Catherine Hogarth, whose father, George—an editor and music critic—had worked with Dickens at the *Chron-icle*. Catherine, 19, was the eldest of several children; two of her sisters, Mary and Georgina, would also play large parts in the novelist's life. The Beadnells, well-tuned to the standards of re-spectable society, could not have been impressed by John Dick-ens' investment portfolio, and the sheer intensity of Charles' enthusiasms—for acting, mak-ing odd jokes, and writing long, facetious poems—very possibly put them off. The Beadnells did not think this oddly asser-tive young stenographer was good enough for Maria. But the arty Hogarths saw him as Boz—an unusually talented young man at the brink of a brilliant career. Besides, as Catherine wrote to one friend, "Mr. Dickens improves very much on acquaintance."

"Mr. Dickens improves very much on acquaintance."
—Catherine Hogarth

But nobody could have quite foreseen the suddenness, or the size, of that success. *Pickwick* had been a routine commission that Dickens had completely made his own. The novel arrived at just the right time—as authors and publishers found new ways to promote and distribute books to a wider range of readers than ever before. Before *The Pickwick Papers*, as A. N. Wilson notes, readers fell basically into two groups. A relatively small constituency—members of "the substantial middle, upper middle, and upper class"—bought "what we should call broadsheet papers or hardback novels." Many more people read popular fiction—romances, adventure stories, comical sketches—"purveyed not in book form but in cheap periodicals, loose paperbacks peddled by traveling salesmen from door to door or at street markets."

Pickwick, appearing every month between light green paper covers, made a direct pitch for the broad base of British readers even as its urbane wit and skillful language made it appealing to all those more educated buyers of broadsheet papers and hardback novels. As Forster recalled, it was probably the novel's comic yet accurate presentation of so many recognizable types, young and old, male and female, that had prompted such widespread delight:

> We had all become suddenly conscious, in the very thick of the extravaganza of adventure and fun set before us, that here were real people. It was not somebody talking humorously about them, but they were there themselves. That a number of persons belonging to the middle and lower ranks of life (Wardles, Winkles, Wellers, Bardells, Snubbinses, Perkers, Bob Sawyers, Dodsons and Foggs) had been somehow added to his intimate and familiar acquaintance, the ordinary reader knew before half a dozen numbers were out; and it took not many more to make clear to the intelligent reader that a new and original genius in the walk of Smollett and Fielding had arisen in England.

Forster

Pickwick became an international bestseller, making Dickens' name in Germany, France, and Russia—where both Tolstoy and Dostoevsky became, in time, admirers. In Britain, the novel's unprecedented success inspired the creation of countless Pickwick-related products, including Pickwick pastries, Pickwick cigars and Sam Weller-style pants. It also prompted imitation among other authors and publishers: William Thackeray's novels, for example, would also appear in monthly serial form.

In late 1836 Dickens quit reporting and, eager to serve his eager audience, began a pattern of almost ceaseless literary activity. Over the next few years Dickens completed *The Pickwick Pa-*

pers while also publishing, in serial form, *Oliver Twist* (1838) and *Nicholas Nickleby* (1838). He also took charge of his first weekly periodical—*Master Humphrey's Clock*—where two more novels, *The Old Curiosity Shop* (1840-41) and *Barnaby Rudge* (1841) first appeared.

These works draw on several traditions—the folk tale, popular theater, and the picaresque novel; they mix satire, sentimentality, and humor in a way that critics of the day recognized as unique. The *Edinburgh Review* likened Dickens to the English painter Hogarth: both show "a keen sense of the ridiculous" and a precise picture of "the ludicrous side of human nature." Dickens, however, did so without resorting to Hogarth's "cynicism and coarseness." Dickens' novels, noted the *Metropolitan Magazine*, are "natural, humorous, and witty in their general character;" they also "rise into pathos, and sometimes, accompanying the immortal soul of man in its loftiest flights, become really sublime." In the midst of this remarkable rise, Dickens' old Chatham schoolmaster, William Giles, sent him a silver snuffbox inscribed "To the Inimitable Boz"—an accolade he relished and often repeated in letters to friends.

Macready

Loss and Gain

In April 1837 Dickens, newly married, moved from sparse bachelor quarters and into a gentleman's townhouse on Doughty Street near fashionable Russell Square. Mary Hogarth—Catherine's younger, unmarried sister—had joined the household to help with childcare, for Charles Culliford Boz Dickens appeared in January 1837, the first of six sons born to Dickens and his wife over the next fifteen years. Two daughters, Mary and Catherine, were born in 1838 and 1839, respectively; both remained close to their father, and Kate, a painter, would later achieve some artistic success of her own.

From the start, however, Dickens was haunted by the past. His parents and, increasingly, his brother Frederick continued to struggle with debt; John Dickens particularly took to cadging money on the strength of his famous son's name. "He, and all of them," Dickens complained, "look upon me as something to be plucked and torn to pieces for their advantage."

Then, in May of 1837, Mary Hogarth, only sixteen, died un-expectedly of heart failure. Dickens was shattered, calling Mary "the grace and life of our home." She was "the dearest friend I ever had," he wrote in one letter, adding elsewhere: "I solemnly believe that so perfect a creature never breathed. I knew her inmost heart and her real worth and value. She had not a fault." For several years after her death, Dickens continued to call Mary "that spirit which directs my life."

The younger Dickens was, by his own account, a roman-tic and an idealist, rather attracted to the notion (often associ-ated with the Victorian era) that women, or at least most of them, were morally superior to men, less prone to brutishness and guile. But Dickens' devotion to Mary, expressed in such fulsome terms, probably points to problems already surfacing in his marriage—an increasingly unhappy union that, in Dickens' view, had brought together two people "in all respects of character and temperament wonderfully unsuited to each other." G. K. Chesterton—who knew as much and as little about this now widely examined mar-riage as anybody else—recalled that Dickens, on the rebound from the Pocket Venus, had met the Hogarths and was suddenly thrown into the society of a whole family of girls.

> I think it does overstate his weakness, and I think it partly con-stitutes his excuse, to say that he fell in love with all of them. As sometimes happens in the undeveloped youth, an abstract feminity simply intoxicated him. And again, I think we shall not be mistakenly accused of harshness if we put the point in this way; that by a kind of accident he got hold of the wrong sister.

Dickens, though, had plenty of distractions from his terrible grief. In the thick of London's literary scene, Dickens' friends and associates included, or would soon include, many of the best-known writers of his age, including Carlyle, Alfred Tennyson, Robert Browning, Walter Savage Landor, Sydney Smith, Leigh Hunt, Francis Jeffrey, Edward Lytton, and Captain Frederick Mar-ryat—the naval officer whose sea novels and adventure stories, now mostly forgotten, were very well-liked in their own day (and, somewhat later, by both Joseph Conrad and Ernest Hemingway).

But by the early 1840s Dickens' closest friends were For-ster, whom he met in 1836, and the actor William Charles Mac-ready, the son of a bankrupt theater manager who became famed for Macbeth and other Shakespearean roles. Dickens and Forster were close in age; Macready was 19 years Dickens' senior. But both men acted as father-figures to Dickens, particularly during the first years of his career. In fact, in certain ways, they both resembled John Dickens: they were volatile, self-dramatizing, and—at least in Macready's case—often morbid and glum. But they also offered examples of disciplined ambition and social influence that Dickens' father could never provide. The tightly wound Macready— who once assaulted a stage manager he found incompetent— played a key role in raising the standards of the British theater, and he pursued his art with a zealous intensity that Dickens well understood. Writes one of Macready's early biographers:

> In Shylock, in order to work himself up to a proper pitch of excitement, Macready, it is said, used to spend some minutes behind the scenes lashing himself into an imaginative rage by cursing *sotto voce*, and shaking violently a ladder fixed against the wall.

Forster's family, from Newcastle, worked in the cattle trade. So he too was a bit of an outsider—another clever, unconnected young provincial pushing his way through the capital with something to prove. Forster was not especially imaginative, but he was smart and industrious, and he promptly set about publishing essays, reviews and, eventually, respectable biographies of Landor and Oliver Goldsmith. Trained in the law, Forster also served Dickens and other artists—including Macready and the poet Robert Browning—on various professional and legal matters. Dickens valued Forster's loyalty and called him "my right hand and cool shrewd head."

But Forster was also bullheaded and combustible; and, like Macready, more widely respected than loved. ("The butcher's boy," his enemies called him.) Dickens, who did love Forster, also found him vexing at times, and probably turned him into the imperious Podsnap in *Our Mutual Friend*. Even a small annoyance could, as Dickens observed, set Forster "smoking all over his head, and fuming himself like a steamboat ready to start."

A Love of Order

Dickens too could be difficult, as friends and family would readily attest. He was obsessed with tidiness and punctuality and—wherever he went—stuck closely to his settled routines: "My love of order," as Dickens called it, governed both his personal and professional affairs. Dickens' daughter Mamie, who adored her father, would nonetheless admit in a memoir that he ran his house rather like a hospital or a battle station, with everything in its place and nothing left to chance. He "made a point of visiting every room in the house once each morning," she recalled, "and if a chair was out of place, or a blind not quite right, or a crumb left on the floor, woe betide the offender!"

Thus Dickens, the sensitive child who grew up amidst much bickering and disorder and daily domestic drama, was absolutely determined not to live with these things as a man. His personal and artistic preoccupation with money also surely derives from the same dark root. He was no Scrooge; Dickens, in fact, rather hated money   hated its crude power and pervasive allure. But he refused to follow his father's path. He would not be underpaid; he would not be exploited; he would not, like his father, beg. He was determined to succeed where his father had failed. It's not surprising that when a young Henry James saw Dickens in the 1860s he was struck by the "automatic hardness" in the man, and his "merciless military eye."

But the poet and essayist Leigh Hunt once noted of Dickens: "What a face is his to meet in a drawing room! It has the life and soul in it of fifty human beings." Dickens, the obsessive-compulsive householder was also an accomplished party thrower and a gracious host. The great disciplinarian was also great fun, joking with friends and treating his children to adventurous holidays. He staged, for family and friends, elaborate plays and magic shows: the Inimitable showed that he really could pull a rabbit of a hat. Dickens, wrote Jane Carlyle, "was the *best* conjuror I ever saw (and I have paid money to see several.)"

Dickens' enthusiasms were wide. He cultivated interests in gardening, dancing, and interior decoration. He taught himself how to play the concertina and to speak Italian and French. He danced the polka and Scottish reels. He kept pets, particularly birds and dogs, and closely studied their habits. He practiced mesmerism.

He was a prolific letter-writer and a popular, accomplished public speaker: his published speeches show the remarkably wide range of his personal interest and charitable concerns. At various times Dickens addressed, in addition to literary and journalistic groups, the Royal Academy, the Metropolitan Sanitary Association, the Artists' Benevolent Fund, the Railway Benevolent Society, the Warehousemen and Clerks' Schools, the Hospital for Sick

Children, and the Metropolitan Rowing Clubs.

Late in the 1830s, Dickens was an integral part of Britain's cultural establishment; he was a member of both the Garrick Club and the new Athenaeum, where he was inducted along with another author of some note—Charles Darwin. In 1839 Dickens moved his growing family and squad of servants to an even more prominent address at One Devonshire Terrace, close to Regent's Park. The large house, which stood until the 1950s, was rather somber-looking, and the Inimitable imitated "the solid but fussy taste of a prosperous Victorian family," as one Dickens biography put it, adding mahogany and rosewood furniture, heavy damask curtains, heavily framed paintings, a marble bust here, a stuffed bird there, and—most notable of all—an indoor WC.

Street in Philadelphia

In 1841 Dickens and Catherine were honored in Edinburgh, where Boz was given Freedom of the City, an honor also granted the Grand Duke Nicholas of Russia and—a year after Dickens—his Royal Highness Prince Albert. This, Forster records, was "the first practical experience of the honors his fame had won for him, and it found him as eager to receive as all were eager to give." A banquet for the young writer drew many of Scotland's leading citizens; to bask in their praise was, Dickens told Forster, almost unreal: "I felt it was very remarkable to see such a number of grey-headed men gathered around my brown flowing locks; and it struck most of those who were present very forcibly." Still, "I was quite self-possessed," Dickens reported, "and, not withstanding the enthoosemoosy, which was very startling, as cool as a cucumber."

In January 1842, Dickens and Catherine boarded a steam ship, the Britannia, and set off on an even grander excursion—to North America, with scheduled stops in Boston, New York, Philadelphia, and Washington, among other eastern locales, as well as St. Louis and Cincinnati out west. Gone for several months,

The Britannia

they left their four children under the joint care of Macready and Catherine's sister Georgina, who would subsequently join the Dickens household and assume her continuing role as governess and, to Dickens himself, a sort of aide-de-camp. Next to Forster, Georgina Hogarth was, for nearly thirty years, Dickens' preferred confidante.

In the United States, Dickens began long-standing friendships with Henry Wadsworth Longfellow, the poet, and Cornelius Felton, a classics professor (and later Harvard president) who, like Dickens, had risen from modest beginnings. Dickens was much impressed by the serene magnificence of the Niagara Falls and the beauty of "the valley of the Susquehannah:" and he was convinced, in the idealistic early days of his visit, that these "warm-hearted" and "frank" and "chivalrous" Americans had, in fact, established a working republic that any progressive-minded European would have to envy. "There is not a man in New England," he reported in one letter, "who has not a blazing fire and a meat dinner every day of his life."

" The raven hasn't more joy in eating a stolen piece of meat, than the American has in reading the English book which he gets for nothing."

20

But the longer he stayed, the less impressed he became. Here, the enthusemoosey was without bounds. Everywhere Dickens was stared at, followed, and rudely interrupted. The press mocked his dandified dress, and called him crass for suggesting, as he often did, that American publishers should abide by the provisions of international copyright and stop flagrantly pirating the works of such British writers as himself.

Some Americans argued that most of the nation's publishers, struggling to establish themselves, couldn't afford to pay fees to English writers who were, after all, making plenty of money in their native countries. But Dickens also detected that "national vanity" made the pleasure of "doing" English writers particularly keen: "it is so dar-nation cute. He has the Englishman so regularly on the hip that his eye twinkles with slyness, cunning, and delight; and he chuckles over the humour of the page with an appreciation of it, quite inconsistent with, and apart from, its honest purchase. The raven hasn't more joy in eating a stolen piece of meat, than the American has in reading the English book which he gets for nothing."

Visited by Spectres

Throughout his journey of seven months, Dickens visited many hospitals, prisons, and schools; as his *American Notes* (1842) makes clear, Dickens was particularly impressed by the Perkins Institution in Boston, where the young Laura Bridgeman, who was both deaf and blind, had already developed impressive communication skills as the result of patient and enlightened instruction. In Lowell, he was similarly impressed by clean, well-run factories where young workers were given many opportunities for self-expression and self-improvement. The English, Dickens believed, had much to learn from these humane and efficient examples.

But he was troubled by the practice of solitary confinement in the penitentiaries of Pennsylvania. Necessarily, Dickens was himself bound to daily bouts of solitude; but when he wasn't writing he looked for company: "the mere record of his conviviality," as Lionel Trilling once put it, "is exhausting." Thus for Dickens, the thought of subjecting any human being, for any reason, to long periods of isolation must be unnatural and cruel. Such isolation, he thought, might also invite spirits, welcome or not—for Dickens, as the scholar Harry Stone wrote, was always alert to "the mysterious murmurings of the invisible world":

> What if ghosts be one of the terrors of the jails? I have pondered on it often, since then. The utter solitude by day and night; the many hours of darkness; the silence of death; the mind for ever brooding on melancholy themes, and having no relief; sometimes an evil conscience very busy: imagine a prisoner covering up his head in the bedclothes and looking out from time to time, with a ghastly dread of some inexplicable silent figure that always sits upon his bed, or stands (if a thing can be said to stand, that never walks as men do) in the same corner of his cell. The more I think of it, the more certain I feel that not a few of these men (during a portion of their imprisonment at least) are nightly visited by spectres.

After returning to England Dickens started focusing on *Martin Chuzzlewit*, his sixth novel. When sales dipped, young Martin Chuzzlewit and his Sam Weller-like companion make the long journey to the United States, where Dickens, who had a very long memory, promptly set out to settle scores, presenting a vivid gallery of Yankee rouges, racists, and boors. Although largely overlooked today, *Martin Chuzzlewit* is a very effective satire further enriched by the presence of Sairey Gamp, the snuff-taking, gin-sipping midwife, and one of Dickens' most memorable grotesques. When Dickens was young, one of his friends praised his ability to "imitate," in "a manner that I have never heard equaled," the working population of London's streets—"whether mere loafers or sellers of fruit, vegetables, or anything else." Mrs. Gamp proves the point.

Dickens' next work of fiction, *A Christmas Carol* (1843) also proved popular even as it pointed to moral themes that would remain prominent in all of his published writings. The story's central character, Ebenezer Scrooge, is selfish and self-absorbed, "solitary as an oyster"—and the embodiment of social assumptions that Dickens would continue to criticize throughout his career. Scrooge doesn't mind that, at Christmas, "want is keenly felt" even as "abundance rejoices." He assumes that, in life, there are winners and losers. The winners should thrive, and the losers—"idle people" he calls them—should die. Scrooge is, of course, rejuvenated in the end, made to confront the toxicity of his views. For years, Scrooge's only business is business, and his ruthless view of life would become known as "social Darwinism" in the years to come.

With *A Christmas Carol,* Dickens' chosen role as a literary moralist—surely the most influential literary moralist of the 19th century—is made indelibly clear. In this story the social gospel is voiced by the jolly, gigantic Ghost of Christmas Present who appears wearing a green robe and, on his head, a "holly wreath" festooned with icicles: he has a "genial face," a "sparkling eye," a "cheery voice" and a "joyful air." "It may be," he warns Scrooge as they stand invisibly in Bob Cratchit's modest house, "that in the sight of Heaven, you are more worthless and less fit to live than millions like this poor man's child." "Pride, ill-will, hatred, envy, bigotry, and selfishness"—the genial Ghost outlines the chief targets in all of Dickens' fiction.

In 1844 Dickens found himself, not for the last time, at loose ends; he felt, as he often did, the impulse to move. This time he took his family to Italy, starting out in Genoa, where he was able to rent the better part of a fine old palace complete with frescoes, fountains, and groves of orange trees. Dickens liked many things about Genoa: the winding streets, the deep blue bay, and the Theatre of Puppets—the Marionetti—that offered "without any exception, the drollest exhibition I ever beheld in my life." But after some months he longed for the larger stimulation of Rome. "Novelty," he wrote, "pleasant to most people, is particularly delightful, I think, to me."

However, as he entered the Eternal City for the first time, Dickens decided that "it looked like—I am half afraid to write the word—like LONDON!!! There it lay, under a thick cloud, with innumerable towers, and steeples, and roofs of houses, rising up into the sky, and high above them all, one Dome."

Of course Rome was not at all like London—a fact that Dickens found both stimulating and disturbing. In his account of his trip, *Pictures From Italy* (1846), Dickens is very much the young English Protestant who is both charmed and appalled by the rites and customs of an old Catholic country that, in his assured view, could promptly use a good dose of modernization. In Rome he struck by the ubiquity of beggars and their "clamorous demands for charity;"

by the presence of coarse-looking monks and ragged priests; by crowded Holy Week observances that tend to strike him as "mere empty forms," degrading and absurd, and much less amusing than the Genovese puppet show.

At St. Peter's he is not at all impressed: "It might be a Pantheon, or a Senate House, or a great architectural trophy, having no other object than architectural triumph." But "there is a black statue of St. Peter, to be sure, under a red canopy, which is larger than life, and which is constantly having its great toe kissed by good Catholics." ("This great painter of English manners," noted *The Economist*, "should bid adieu to politics and controversy—should cease to paint pictures of Italy—a land which he does not understand—and confine himself to London and Middlesex.")

A Voice of Progress

While in Naples, Dickens fulfilled a long-held ambition of climbing Mount Vesuvius. As Arthur Adrian relates in *Georgina Hogarth and the Dickens Circle*, he planned the excursion to the volcano with his usual mixture of theatricality and care, hiring an armed guard, a dozen guides, and six saddle horses. The party, which also included Catherine and Georgina, started out on their way just before dusk, hoping to watch the sunset and to observe "the raging fire of the crater by dark."

The climb was arduous and steep. Dickens' companions "scarcely dared steal a downward glance at the fearful chasm behind them." Near the top, the smoke thickened, and the group, gasping and choking, stopped. One guide, watching Boz climb on alone, screamed in dismay, "tearing his hair like a madman," as Dickens himself would cheerfully relate. At the top, Dickens stared deep into the crater and then clambered down, "singed but safe." The group's descent, writes Adrian, proved no less dangerous—and equally revealing of what life with Boz was often like:

Supported by half a dozen men, the two women faltered down the narrow track gouged into the ice and snow. Suddenly Georgina, between Dickens and the head guide, froze to feel a jerk as the latter lost his footing and plunged into the blackness, followed by a shrieking Italian boy and another Guide carrying spare cloaks. Shaken, she and Catherine inched on, their garments in torn disarray. Not until midnight was their exhaustive ordeal ended. By then the head guide and the boy, both painfully injured, had been rescued; but the third victim—Dickens's cloak with him—was still missing the next morning. 'My Ladies are the wonder of Naples,' Dickens boasted,' and everybody is open-mouthed.'

,

Back in London, brimming with energy, Dickens joined other investors—including the railroad magnate Joseph Paxton—in the funding of a national newspaper, the *Daily News*. Dickens, the designated editor, set about hiring some of the best reporters and editors in London who were committed to "the advocacy of all rational and honest means by which wrong might be redressed, just right maintained, and the happiness and welfare of society promoted."

This meant the paper would oppose, for example, "Corn Laws" that taxed grain imports to the benefit of the implacable land-owning class that was often the object of Dickens' political satire. Dickens also wanted the *Daily News* to call

for more and better schools for the poor; to support the growing "sanitary movement" that focused on the pollution of the Thames and the resultant spread of disease; to condemn the continued use of public executions, and the mob excitement they inevitably aroused. He also wanted to give his father a steady job. Thus "the governor," as Dickens called him, was hired to supervise the parlia mentary reporters, for like Wilkins Micawber he brought a certain keeness to the many jobs he could never quite hold. (One of the paper's staff would later describe John Dickens as "full of fun," "never given much to locomotion" and "fond of a glass of grog.")

Dickens, though, soon grew tired of the stress and burden of the *Daily Noose*, as he now called it; within weeks he quit the post, passed it on to Forster, and went to work on his next novel, *Dombey and Son*. In key respects *Dombey* amplifies *A Christmas Carol*. The title character, Paul Dombey, is a Scrooge-like figure who, after much emotional suffering, finds himself chastened and able to perceive the world afresh. But the book is more subtle and more character-driven than any of Dickens' previous fictions. *Dombey* and its successor, *David Copperfield*, signal a decisive turn in the direction of Dickens' art—henceforth, comedy and complexity live more closely side by side.

Dickens never wrote another comic romp like *Pickwick*, but

in 1850 he did return to journalism as part owner and "conductor" of a weekly magazine, *Household Words.* The publication wasn't unique: other well-known writers, including Dickens' friend Captain Marryat, had fronted popular magazines that mixed serial fiction with commentary, feature stories, and personal essays. Dickens, however, brought his perfectionism and his brilliant literary sensibility to this project. He hired a first-rate journalist, W. H. Wills, to be his assistant. Still, Dickens generally read, edited, and often thoroughly rewrote all submissions to *Household Words.* This practice flattered some contributors, peeved others, and most importantly ensured the publication's quality and popularity. *Household Words* was a hit from the start, and—as similar publications came and went—its circulation and influence remained steady and strong.

Household Words Office, Wellington Street, Strand

A Fever

Dickens' activities as an editor did not compromise his literary activities. In 1852, Dickens wrote and published *Bleak House,* one of his most critically acclaimed novels—a work of searing satire, carefully wrought and highly symbolic. *Bleak House* targets abuses in the Court of Chancery, and a legal establishment that, in Dickens' view, was a sort of sinister cult less devoted to the administration of justice than to the perpetuation of its own arrogant power. *Bleak House* is bleaker than *Dombey and Son,* despite the presence of Esther Summerson, its sympathetic narrator; it presents a world view that is quite dark in a recognizably modern way, informed by elements of the grotesque and the absurd.

The critic and novelist Walter Allen might have been thinking of *Bleak House* when he observed that when we read Dickens, "we very soon realize we are in the presence of anything but the common vision of life; we have been, as it were, plumped down at the centre of a mind that sees and experiences life in a way quite other than that which we agree to think of as the normal, a mind that exists all the time at a pitch of intensity the rest of us only attain in nightmare or in fever."

In 1851 Dickens moved his family once more, taking lease of an even larger house in Bloomsbury, on Tavistock Square. Once again, Dickens remodeled much of the place to meet his exacting standards, converting a large schoolroom in the rear of the house into a small theatre, complete with "proper footlights, proper scenery, proper curtain—in fact no expense or trouble was spared to make the whole thing complete," as one associate recalled. Dickens also added the latest in plumbing advancements —a shower bath. This was necessary, the author explained in a letter, "because my cut-out way of life obliges me to be so much upon the strain, that I think it is of service to me as a refresher—not as a taker out, but as a putter in of energy."

London still energized Dickens' imagination. But he also found it increasingly hard to take.The city, growing fast, was also becoming crowded, dirty, and unsafe. London in the 1850s, as one historian writes, was "becoming increasingly intolerable, with fog in winter, stench in summer, and all the year round, the lurking fear of cholera. The smell from the Thames was so offensive that the Honourable Members hung gauze soaked in disinfectant at the Windows of the House of Commons."

During the 1840s Dickens had regularly fled from the city by leasing a house in the village of Broadstairs, beside the sea, in Kent. As his 1851 essay, "Our Watering-Place" suggests, Dickens was quite at home in this unpretentious place, with its bracing air, its slow pace and quirky charms. In the municipal library, "a large doll, with movable eyes, was put up to be raffled for, by five-and-twenty members at two shillings, seven years ago this autumn, and the list is not full yet."

In the 1850s, however, he found himself increasingly drawn to Boulogne-Sur-Mer, the old fishing port and tourist town just south of Calais. Dickens salutes Boulogne in an 1854 essay in "Our French Watering-Place." He delights in the hard-working fishermen, with their bright red caps, and in the robust loveliness of the fishermen's wives, who walk barefoot, lugging huge baskets of fish. They have "the finest legs ever carved by Nature in the brightest mahogany, and they walk like Juno." In Boulogne, Dickens formed friendships with local tradesmen and hoteliers—

including the simple but straightforward M. Loyal, who "is of a highly convivial temperament, and his hospitality is unbounded." M. Loyal is, in key ways, Charles Dickens' Ideal Man: "Under blouse or waistcoat, he carries one of the gentlest hearts that beat in a nation of gentle people."

À la d'Orsay

Dickens friendships were notably diverse. These included John Elliotson, a professor of medicine at the University of London who became much admired for his teaching skills and, later, much mocked for his zealous support of mesmerism, phrenology, and other unorthodox forms of medical treatment and research. Another of Dickens' friends, the archeologist Austen Layard, had led several major excavations in Iraq, and described them in his popular 1849 book *Nineveh and its Remains*. Later, Layard entered Parliament as a Liberal, and he earned Dickens' strong support when he spearheaded attacks on governmental incompetence and corruption. For Dickens and Layard, the Crimean War was, in its handling, too symptomatic of the way Britain's political leaders conducted business: it was poorly planned and indifferently administered, and it enriched those who, well-briefed in the reigning patterns of corruption, knew too well how to grease the wheels.

Dickens worked even more closely and more frequently with Angela Burdett-Coutts, the rather reclusive banking heiress who became not only one of the richest people in Britain, but one of the greatest philanthropists of the Victorian age. Convinced that God had given her this £ 2 million-pound inheritance to do good in the world, Burdett-Coutts devoted her life to supporting a remarkably wide range of charitable causes. She funded schools and housing estates for the poor, and she helped start what became the Royal Society for the Prevention of Cruelty to Animals. Dickens and Coutts shared the belief that, in most cases, charity should be used to help people help themselves; thus Coutts also underwrote many small-business ventures in Britain and throughout the colonies; and, with Dickens' assistance, she established Urania Cottage, a home in Shepherd's Bush for young women seeking to give up prostitution and related lives of crime. Theologically, Coutts was more conservative than Dickens, and he took pains to persuade her that the cottage's residents— "these tarnished and battered images of God," as he called them—not be browbeaten with threats of damnation. Their chaplain should be "imbued" with "great, merciful, Christian thoughts," Dickens urged, "guided only by "the New Testament." "I am confident," he adds, "that harm is done to this class of minds by the injudicious use of the Old."

Dickens was also a great friend of Count Alfred d'Orsay— the French military officer, painter, and bon vivant who was quite clearly not, like Coutts, an evangelical Christian. D'Orsay was well-known throughout London for his impeccable manners and flamboyant dress: Carlyle called him the "Phoebus Apollo of dandyism." Reputedly, d'Orsay sported scented dogskin gloves and sometimes employed a boy to stand by and light his cigars; he also served as a godfather to Dickens' fourth son—the luminously named Alfred d'Orsay Tennyson Dickens. (Five other Dickens boys bore the names of their father's literary friends and heroes: Walter Landor, Francis Jeffrey, Sydney Smith, Henry Fielding and Edward Bulwer-Lytton. Not surprisingly, perhaps, none took up writing careers of their own.)

Many of Dickens' friends paid tribute to his sociability and generosity, and took his affections and idiosyncrasies in good stride. Thus the writer Mary Boyle recalled Tavistock House and its vast drawing room with special affection; it was "replete to me with memories of innumerable evenings passed in the most congenial and delightful intercourse; dinners, where the guests vied with each other in brilliant conversation, whether intellectual, witty, or sparkling—evenings devoted to music or theatricals." At Tavistock House "we danced in the New Year. It seemed like a page cut out of *A Christmas Carol* as far as fun and frolic went: authors, actors, friends from near and far, formed the avenues of two long English country dances."

Edward Bulwer-Lytton

But privately, Thomas Huxley called Dickens a snob, and other observers, including some of his friends, quietly made fun of his children's names, his lavish parties, and his own dandified manner of dress, which often included velvet collars, bright colors, sizable rings and other bits of jewelry that, in today's parlance, might qualify as bling. Thus Carlyle, who sometimes spoke patronizingly of Dickens, once noted that he was "dressed a la d'Orsay rather than well." For Thackeray, certainly, Dickens' style revealed that he was not, alas, a gentleman, but an *arriviste*—his flashy displays too typical of the *nouveaux riches*.

It's A Battlefield

Dickens was not umble. Instead—as his protégé Edmund Yates once noted—he "was imperious in the sense that his life was conducted on the *sic volo sic jubeo* principle, and that everything gave way before him." Moreover, in a class-bound society, Dickens, as Forster observed, "would take as much pains to keep out of the houses of the great as others take to get into them" Dickens despised the sort of fawning around socially powerful people that he observed in other writers—including his sometime friend, Thackeray. Dickens' 1855 essay, "The Toady Tree" lambastes the persistent influence, in all aspects of British society, of the coarse and indifferent rich, and it mocks those "toadies" who, whether for vanity or financial gain, continue to curry their favor. Dickens knows too many people who would, for example, "rather exchange nods with a semi-idiotic dowager, than fraternize with another Shakespeare."

As Edmund Wilson wrote, Dickens' "behavior toward Society, in the capitalized sense, was rebarbative to the verge of truculence; he refused to learn its patter and its manners; and his satire on the fashionable world comes to figure more and more prominently in his novels." Dickens, as Wilson put it, "is one of the very small group of British intellectuals to whom the opportunity has been offered to be taken up by the governing class and who have actually declined that honor."

But then, the sheer size of Dickens' success really had put him in a class by himself: "If I went to a new colony," he once observed, "I would force myself to the top of the social milk-pot, and live upon the cream." Another protégé, Percy Fitzgerald, observed decades after Dickens' death that:

He was a figure in the State. It is really impossible to give an idea of his attraction. His books were public assets: each green-coated number as it came out was devoured by an admiring community. And this particularly should be borne in mind: that all his special quips and humors were then utter novelties— such as had never been heard before; now, after fifty or sixty years' reading, we are all accustomed to them. His sayings were all taken into common talk and became proverbial (the father of a family, perhaps, being named in the home circle 'The Aged P.') Nowadays we can hardly realize this. We have nobody of such magic temperament to look to.

Although he excelled in his public role, Dickens was less frequently as cool as a cucumber in his private life. Starting in the late 1840s, Dickens' letters begin to reveal a growing sense of general discomfort and anxiety. He finds himself more frequently than before unable to concentrate. He reveals that he could barely look at one of his books-in-progress, but "dodged at it, like a bird at a lump of sugar." He can't sleep. He hears "hypochondrical whisperings." He goes "wandering about at night into the strangest places"—"seeking rest, and finding none." Half-seriously, he considers moving to Australia or New Zealand to start a magazine. He wants to be a vagabond: "I loathe domestic hearths." More and more he thinks of the "one happiness I have missed in life, and one friend and companion I have never made."

Charles Dickens as he appeared reading

There is, moreover, a painful recognition of mortality during this period, as a long series of serious and fatal illnesses came to members of his family and friends. Tuberculosis was one real threat, and cholera another. In 1851 Charles and Catherine lost their infant daughter, Dora. In the same year John Dickens submitted to serious bladder surgery, without anesthesia—a brave but fatal act that his son duly hailed. In his correspondence Dickens alludes more frequently to unending work and inevitable exhaustion; life, he perceives, is "a fight," necessarily a test of strength and endurance for all. It's a battlefield, and Dickens straps on his "armour" and carries on.

31

A Life on Stage

For better or worse, it was always Dickens' way to find distraction and refreshment in a whirl of intense activities: writing, travelling and—increasingly—acting. In the autumn of 1845 Dickens decided to pull together an amateur production of *Every Man in His Humor,* the Ben Jonson comedy that he believed resembled his own early fiction—not least in the use of comic characters who exemplified large temperamental traits or "humors." Dickens worked out every detail of the production, initially held in a small London theatre, and he took the role of the braggart Bobadil for himself. The choleric Forster played Kitely and several other writers—including *Punch* humorists Douglas Jerrold and the sanguine Mark Lemon—also took parts. Dickens hired a tailor from the English Opera House to design the costumes, and his friend Clarkson Stanfield, a leading artist, to paint the scenery. Thus what began as a lark for Dickens became, inevitably, an extravaganza. For the rest of his life Dickens took every opportunity to be where he now felt most fully at home—on stage.

He oversaw more performances of *Every Man in His Humor* and its alternate—*The Merry Wives of Windsor.* The great Macready was not much impressed by the labored earnestness that these amateur actors brought to their parts—but Dickens, he conceded, could be quite convincing in his way. These stagings were generally accompanied by farces, as was the custom of the day; in these Dickens, who was slight, teamed up with Lemon, who was not, to great applause. In *Love, Law, and Physic* Dickens and Lemon were, in the words of one spectator, "hand in glove in inventing liberties that lifted the farce to heights of absurdity." Together, they also performed another crowd-pleaser, *Used Up,* for which Lemon "invented a special laugh," a "squeaking, hysterical giggle followed by a suddenly checked gasp. Dickens loved it and begged Lemon to do it over and over again."

In the summer of 1848, Dickens took his productions of Jonson and Shakespeare up north to Manchester, Liverpool, Birmingham, and Glasgow. As always, the halls were packed and the crowds enthusiastic. Although he sometimes complained of "the protracted agonies of management," Dickens clearly relished every aspect of this demanding work, and his enthusiasm was often passed on to the cast. The performances were followed by parties, where—as Norman and Jeanne Mackenzie record—Dickens stirred up the punch and arranged the entertainment, including word quizzes and games of leapfrog. "I never saw anything like those clever men," observed one bystander as he watched Dickens and his fellow actors bound over each other's backs. "They're just for all the world like a parcel of boys!"

In 1850, Dickens joined with Edward ("It was a dark and stormy night") Bulwer in the establishment of a Guild of Literature and Art, which aimed mainly to raise an endowment for the support of notable writers who had slipped into poverty. Again, Dickens assembled his cast and, in London and elsewhere, performed Bulwer's *Not So Bad As We Seem*, a costume drama featuring lots of in-jokes and characters with names like "Mr. Softhead" and "Hardman." It is, in part, about class consciousness and social climbing, and it's actually not as bad as you might think, coming from the pen of Edward Bulwer-Lytton. Dickens plays the part of John Wilmot, an apparently rakish figure named after the notorious Earl of Rochester. At one point Wilmot observes: "I delight in odd characters."

The cast of *Not So Bad as We Seem* would also include Forster, Jerrold, the novelist Wilkie Collins, and the painter Augustus Egg. It too was an amateur production with firm professional standards and the accompanying support of carpenters, dressers, property-men, tailors, and barbers. This Charles Dickens production also drew large audiences and raised huge funds as it played in and outside of London—in Bristol, Bath, Liverpool and elsewhere. After an 1852 performance in Manchester, Dickens wrote to Bulwer-Lytton: "I cannot tell you what a triumph we have had. I have been so happy in all this that I could have cried."

The Stage
Lover

Must be Amused

And so, even as he supervised a weekly magazine and struggled with the composition of his increasingly complex fiction, Dickens spent more and more time as a public performer. In December 1853, aiming to raise funds for an "industrial and literary institute" in Birmingham, Dickens gave a series of public readings from *A Christmas Carol* and his other seasonal stories. For years Dickens had toyed with the idea of giving public readings, but he assumed that—among members of the literary establishment at least—such appearances would be considered *infra dig*. But this, he decided, was an effectively direct way to raise funds for worthy causes. Besides, Peter Ackroyd writes, "he loved to hold an audience spellbound; he loved the gaslight and the melodrama; he loved, in other words, to be taken out of ordinary reality into some bright and coherent world of the imagination."

And he was good. Once, Thomas Carlyle went to hear Dickens read from *The Pickwick Papers*. It was the famous trial scene, and—as always—Dickens not only read with brio, but in the voices of his characters. As he brought forth the personalities of Pickwick and Mrs. Bardell, the formidable Carlyle, not known for his cheerfulness, began laughing so hard that, according to one witness, "he fairly exhausted himself" and, at intermission, required the steadying influence of a brandy-and-water. "Charley," he gasped between sips, "you carry a whole company of actors under your hat."

> *"I have no relief but in action. I am incapable of rest. I am quite confident I should rust, break, and die if I spared myself. Much better to die, doing."*

Dickens' stage career heated up even as some of his older friendships were cooling down. He began to see far less of Forster, who in addition to his own literary activities had taken a government position on the Lunacy Commission—a post that required frequent inspection tours of various "lunatic-asylums," as they were called, and the writing of related reports. Forster had also married, leaving Dickens to seek the company of other, equally restless and generally younger men-about-town, including Collins, who wrote regularly for *Household Words* and is today best-known for his bestselling novels *The Woman in White* (1858) and *The Moonstone* (1868). As their correspondence shows, the more bohemian Collins was more willing, at a moment's notice, to join Dickens for "a bellyful of punch" or a night at the theater.

Dickens spent much of 1854 working on *Hard Times*, a satirical novel that draws on labor tensions that were growing in Preston and other parts of the industrial north. Dedicated to Carlyle, *Hard Times* reveals much about Dickens' more mature political attitudes as it offers vivid portraits of the types of men he had always conveyed with ridicule and scorn. There is Gradgrind, the "inflexible, dry, and dictatorial" schoolmaster oblivious to the life-enriching power of the imagination. There is Hart-house, the spoiled and monied politician who has no principles and is so devoid of honest wonder and delight that he finds all of life a bore. And there is Bounderby, an updated depiction of Scrooge—the banker and industrialist who finds pleasure in his own imagined superiority and in dismissing the needs of the great legions of working poor who, he insists, want only to be coddled, and "fed on turtle soup and venison, with a gold spoon."

Against this grim lot Dickens places the more vital members of Sleary's circus—a band of itinerant entertainers who fly and tumble through life with no motive of self-promotion or greedy gain. The stout and lisping Sleary, despite his "flabby surface" and "muddled head which was never quite sober and never drunk," prompts Dickens' admiration because he and his performers have readily embraced the task of bringing a bit of color and pleasure to a rough, grey world.

Parisian Cockneys

After finishing *Hard Times*, Dickens moved to Paris, leasing an apartment near the Champs-Elysees. As in Boulogne, Dickens felt very much at home in Paris, where his books were enormously popular and where he took readily to the city's bright and incomparable pleasures—the restaurants, theatres, and the intellectual company. Dickens' French friends and acquaintances included Victor Hugo, Eugéne Sue, Alphonse de Lamartine, and the actor Charles Fechter—one of the few artistic contemporaries to win Dickens' complete and unqualified praise.

The journalist George Sala, another *Household Words* regular, would fondly recall how, in the mid 1850s, Dickens would often meet up with other English artists and literary men—"Anglo-Parisian Bohemian Cockneys"—who were similarly "travelling backwards and forwards between London and the Gay City, and taking rooms in the Quartier Latin on the Rue de Seine, on what we used to call the 'Surrey side of the river.'" (In 1850, as Dickens' essay "A Flight" relates, the South Eastern Railway had introduced a "Double Special Express Service" that reduced the London-to-Paris route to a relatively easy twelve hours' journey.)

"When Dickens was in Paris," wrote Sala, "I lived for a while in clover. We used to dine at Véfour's or at the Trois Frères Provencaux, in the Palais Royale; and afterwards I would accompany him to the Porte St-Martin or to the Vaudeville Theater: he paying all the costs and charges in his accustomed hearty and liberal manner."

In Paris, Dickens worked hard on his sixth novel, *Little Dorrit*, which reinvokes the presence of John Dickens even as it expands on political themes that inform *Bleak House* and *Hard Times*. Much of the book is set in the Marshalsea, where the weak and egotistical Dorrit wastes away his years while basking in the care of his youngest daughter, Amy. Another character, Arthur Clennam, is a "grave dark man" who enters middle age still hampered by the effects of a bad childhood. The adults in his world embodied, in their way, the same toxic prejudices that distort the lives of Gradgrind and Bounderby: they are cramped fools who take their pleasure in the suffocation of more vital souls.

Little Dorrit also reveals Dickens' still-simmering anger with civic corruption and governmental incompetence; he offers, in the Circumlocution Office, a very precise symbol of the insolence of the government that purports to serve the public's needs. There are wonderful comic characters and moments in *Little Dorrit,* but not enough for some critics who believed that Dickens was spending too much time ridiculing civil structures and ignoring the rare gifts that had brought him fame. "As a humorist," observed the conservative *Blackwood's Magazine,* "we prefer Dickens to all living men. But as artist, moralist, politician, philosopher and ultra-philanthropist, we prefer many living men, women, and children to Dickens."

While working on *Little Dorrit,* Dickens allowed, in a letter to Forster, that he was "never at rest, and never satisfied, and ever trying after something that is never reached, and to be always laden with plot and plan and care and worry." And so once again Dickens decided to mount a play in his Tavistock House Theater. This was *The Frozen Deep,* Wilkie Collins' three-act melodrama based broadly on Sir John Franklin's arctic explorations.

Once again, Dickens supervised every aspect of the production and—like the great Macready—he prepared scrupulously for his role. Dickens played Richard Wardour, the jealous but ultimately noble rival of Collins' character, Frank Aldersly. Dickens rehearsed outdoors at Gad's Hill, his country home in Kent, tramping through fields, declaiming his speeches to the startled amusement of the nearby villagers.

Inevitably, *The Frozen Deep* opened in a London theater, its goal the raising of funds for the family of the writer Douglas Jerrold, recently deceased. *The Frozen Deep* attracted Queen Victoria

Mutton Broth.

The best part of the mutton from which to make good broth is the chump end of the loin, but it may be made excellently from the scrag end of the neck only, which should be stewed gently for a long time (full three hours or longer, if it be large) until it becomes tender, but not boiled to rags as it usually is; a few grains of whole pepper, with a couple of fried onions and some turnips, should be put along with the meat an hour or two before sending up the broth, which should be strained from the vegetables, and chopped parsley and thyme be mixed in it; the turnips should be mashed and served in a separate dish to be eaten with the mutton, with parsley-and-butter or caper sauce. If meant for persons in health, it ought to be strong or it will be insipid; the cooks usually skim it frequently, but if given as a remedy for a severe cold, it is much better not to remove the fat, as it is very healing to the chest.

— from Catherine Dickens,
What Shall we Have for Dinner?

among other notables; and, once again, Dickens felt compelled to take the production on the road, heading north once more, where he would fill halls in Liverpool, Manchester, and Birmingham. This time, however, Dickens decided to round out the cast with professional actors, including the eighteen-year-old Ellen Ternan. "Nelly," as she was called, came from a family of well-known troupers: her mother had appeared on stage with the great Macready himself.

A Quest

As the world now knows, Dickens fell in love with Ellen Ternan. She was both worldly and respectable, headstrong and smart—more Bella Wilfour than Dora Spenlow. Initially, writing to close friends, Dickens joked about his infatuation, comparing himself to a knight on a chivalric quest. But Ellen, he soon decided, embodied a revitalizing ideal he could not live without. "Too late to say, put a curb on," he told Forster, "and don't rush at hills. I have no relief but in action. I am incapable of rest. I am quite confident I should rust, break, and die if I spared myself. Much better to die, doing. What I am in that way, nature made me first, and my way of life has of late, alas! confirmed."

Ellen Ternan

In 1858 Dickens and Catherine separated. She moved to a home in Regent's Park, and he retreated to Gad's Hill Place, a pretty, unpresupposing estate he had recently purchased near Rochester, close to his boyhood home. From the start, Dickens seemed less keenly interested in denying his relationship with Ellen Ternan than in halting rumors, traced to Catherine's mother, that he had actually been having a long-term affair with Georgina Hogarth, his devoted sister-in-law. Dickens was so angry that he issued a fervent if vague denial on the front page of *Household Words*. In it, he referred to "some domestic trouble of mine, of long-standing" and to how this trouble "has been made the occasion of misrepresentations, most grossly false, most monstrous, and most cruel." This circuitous self-defense only prompted more curiosity about his personal affairs.

Dickens' later writings perhaps are, as some critics suggest, full of self-scrutiny and guilt; after all, both *Our Mutual Friend* and *The Mystery of Edwin Drood* feature characters wearing disguises and leading double lives. Still, it's also possible to detect rising elements of anger and resentment as well: Dickens, who repeatedly attacked hypocrisy in his fiction, clearly resented the immense presence of social conventions that not only forced him to remain in his unhappy marriage, but compelled him to hide Ellen Ternan away. But she was hidden, at times, in plain sight. The two often travelled together quite openly. And Dickens listed her prominently in his will.

Dickens' affair, and his separation from Catherine, ended or strained many old friendships (with Mark Lemon, for example, and Angela Burdett Coutts.) And because of it, Dickens feuded with his long-standing publishers, Bradbury and Evans. In a great fit of pique he closed *Household Words,* which Bradbury and Evans published, and introduced *All The Year Round*, with Chapman and Hall. *All the Year Round* was also a strong success for many years, its sales buoyed along the way by the serialization of two of Dickens' most popular novels—*A Tale of Two Cities* and *Great Expectations.*

In *A Tale of Two Cities*, set during the French Revolution, Dickens again trains his guns on an obtuse ruling elite that was, he believed, ultimately at fault for most social sins and civic distortions. *Great Expectations* allowed him to tell his own story once more, in a veiled and serio-comic manner and to salute again, through Joe Gargery, the virtues of unqualified kindness and selflessness that he most admired but did not himself possess in such a ready, instinctive way.

Walking Fast

"I hold my inventive capacity," Dickens once wrote, "on the stern condition that it must master my own life, often have complete possession of me, make its own demands upon me, and sometimes for months together, put everything else away from me." But for years he managed to balance out his mental exertions with a vigorous regimen of physical exercise. Dickens was a prodigious walker, covering many miles each day; the peripatetic Sala, for one, as Forster notes, "has described himself encountering Dickens in the oddest places and most inclement weather, in Ratcliffe Highway, on Haverstock Hill, on Camberwell Green, in Gray's Inn Lane, in the Wandsworth Lane Road, at Hammersmith Broadway, in Norton Folgate, and at Kensal New Town." "'A hansom whirled you by the Bell and Horns at Brompton,'" Forster records Sala as saying, "'and there he was striding, as with seven-league boots, seemingly in the direction of North End, Fulham. The Metropolitan Railway sent you forth at Lisson Grove, and you met him plodding speedily towards the Yorkshire Stingo. He was to be met rapidly skirting the grim wall of the prison in Coldbath Fields, or trudging along the Seven Sisters Road at Holloway, or bearing, under a steady press of sail, underneath Highgate Archway, or pursuing the even tenor of his way up the Vauxhall Bridge Road.'"

But starting in the late 1850s, it became obvious to all that Dickens' health was not good. His walking habit was combined with the dangerous diet of a wealthy Victorian; in fact, an 1851 cookbook published by Catherine Dickens (as Lady Maria Clutterbuck) reveals that, in the Dickens household, mutton chops, cream sauces, and toasted cheese were often on the menu. Dickens smoked cigars and suffered often from sleeplessness and from sharp pains in his side. In later years he was often dizzy, short of breath, and plagued by cramping pains in his lower legs and feet. Reading the symptoms, William Ober, a physician and literary critic, once suggested that "it's very likely that Dickens was hypertensive, though the sphygmomanometer had not yet been invented."

Catherine Hogarth Dickens

In early June 1865 Dickens nearly perished when the train in which he and Ellen Ternan were riding jumped the tracks at Staplehurst, between Dover and London, killing several and injuring many more. At the scene of the wreck, Dickens calmly assisted Ellen and other injured passengers. But the incident shook him badly and only heightened a sense of anxiety that, as his letters to Forster and others reveal, was now a constant factor in his life. Dickens complained of vision problems, a certain "faintness of heart," a sharp "pain in the ball of my left eye," and—during or after a public reading—a "curious feeling of soreness all round the body—which I suppose to arise from the great exertion of voice." Dickens did not completely avoid doctors, but he was, not surprisingly, inclined to seek his own course of diagnosis and relief: "a dozen oysters and a little champagne," he reported on one occasion, "constitute the best restorative I have yet tried."

Dickens was roundly urged to moderate his activities; he was, after all, rich, and the owner of a fine country home where, as Forster and others pointed out, he could easily very easily settle into a squire's life of writing and moderate exercise. Dickens did enjoy tramping about the countryside with his loyal contingent of dogs, and some photographs taken during his final years show him settled peacefully on the lawn or in a garden chair, book in hand. At Gad's Hill Dickens wrote *Our Mutual Friend* (1865), his final completed novel and an ambitious critique of the culture of money; and, the unfinished *Mystery of Edwin Drood* (1870), a mystery novel that takes its readers into London's opium dens among other exotic places, and that is marked throughout by the sort of dark colors also found in *Our Mutual Friend*.

Still, in 1867 Dickens insisted in travelling again to America, lured by the blandishments of promoters; by the implication that he could be, in effect, the next Jenny Lind—the "Swedish Nightingale" who, in the 1850s, had filled theatres across the land. This time, then, Dickens went not as a rising young celebrity on a public holiday, but as the world's most famous novelist, a true household name, whose talents as a performer had been everywhere acclaimed. Accordingly, Dickens made far fewer sight-seeing trips, and he steered clear of the old and still largely unresolved issue of international copyright law. This time Dickens travelled as the star of a wholly new form of entertainment: the literary one-man show.

The predictions proved right. In the States, as in Britain, Dickens' performances always sold out. People stood in line for hours—and even days—for tickets, covering themselves in blankets against the cold. This time around, however, Dickens badly missed Ellen Ternan, and he was often ill. But he was cheered everywhere, and in turn he roundly congratulated the Americans for the many noticeable improvements in their civic and cultural life. He went home with £20,000—a sizable portion of his final estate.

Back in England, as he worked on *Drood*, Dickens carried on with another round of readings which he had freshened up with material from, among other works, *Oliver Twist*. Forster and others urged him not to persist in enacting the scene in which Bill Sikes bludgeons poor Nancy and leaves her dead in a pool of blood; it was too intense, they warned, prompting some in the audience to scream and faint. Moreover, it left Dickens drained, his pulse racing. But Dickens was determined: playing the parts of David Copperfield and Chops, the Dwarf, was not enough. He must be Bill Sikes too.

Dickens died suddenly, at 58, on June 9,1870—the fifth anniversary of the Staplehurst train crash. Most biographers, following Forster, have understandably concluded that Dickens had wrecked himself physically, intentionally or not. It's curious to note, however, that the author's eldest son, Charley, who did not share his father's manic tendencies, "succumbed," as Arthur Adrian notes, "to an apoplectic attack similar to his father's," at the age of 59. Of Dickens' nine children to reach adulthood, only two—Katey and Henry—lived into old age.

In his will, Dickens insisted "that I be buried in an inexpensive, unostentatious, and strictly private manner; that no public announcement be made of the time or place of my burial; that at utmost not more than three plain mourning coaches be employed; and that those who attend my funeral wear no scarf, cloak, black bow, long hat-band, or other such revolting absurdity."

Dickens was buried in Westminster Abbey in Poets' Corner, the figure of Shakespeare looking down. The funeral service itself, on June 14, was limited to family members and friends; a simple stone marks his place. Five days later, a public service was held in the Abbey, with Dean Stanley presiding. He chose his reading from the Gospel of Luke, the parable of Lazarus and the rich man.

Forster's biography stretched to three bestselling volumes that appeared between 1872 and 1874. His account of Dickens' impoverished childhood was a real revelation; but some reviewers decided that they didn't like the complicated subject of Forster's book nearly as much as the dashing, laughing, inimitable Boz they remembered, and whose image they sought to preserve. Other critics complained that Forster's book was poorly organized, more memoir than biography, and too padded out by long extracts from Dickens' letters. Forster, they implied, had simply opened a drawer and copied out lengthy extracts from the correspondence he maintained with Dickens over many years. Forster did, however, also include this note from "an American gentleman" who, while working with a team of surveyors in the Sierra Nevada mountains, came across a small hut miles from anywhere. Its occupant, he told Forster, came forth into the cold "to hail us and solicit whiskey and tobacco. He was dressed in a suit made entirely of flour-sacks, and was curiously labeled on various parts of his person *Best Family Flour. Extra.* His head was covered by a wolf's skin drawn from the brute's head—with ears standing erect in a fierce alert manner."

> He was a most extraordinary object, and told us he had not seen a human being in four months. He lived on bear and elk meat and flour, laid in during his short summer. Emigrants in the season paid him a kind of ferry-toll. I asked him how he passed the time, and he went to a barrel and produced Nicholas Nickleby and Pickwick. I found he knew them almost by heart. He did not know, or seem to care, about the author; but he gloried in Sam Weller, despised Squeers, and would probably have taken the latter's scalp with great skill and cheerfulness.

For Forster, of couse, this anecdote was meant to highlight Dickens' unmatched appeal. But in the coming decades, it probably did not help lift Dickens' stock within the Bloomsbury Circle or among a newer generation of critics and intellectuals who found Dickens too dated for their tastes. He was a literary moralist and a comedian with a sentimental streak and a melodramatic side who did not seem relevant to a new generation of modernist writers who sought to distance themselves not only from the sort of literary populism that Dickens embraced, but from a span of attitudes and conventions that defined the Victorian Age. Thus Virginia Woolf once admitted that while she would happily go through life as Shakespeare's cat, she wouldn't go across the street to meet Charles Dickens.

By the late 1930s, however, Dickens' critical reputation was very much on the rise, helped particularly by two influential writers—George Orwell and Edmund Wilson. Orwell conceded that Dickens had limitations as a realistic writer; that his political thinking was at times contradictory and vague. But then, he wasn't after literary realism and his eye—for the telling detail, the arresting comic touch—was simply unequaled by any previous writer of narrative prose. Moreover, at a time when Fascism and Communism had risen with murderous and catastrophic results, Dickens' political stance appeared more and more relevant and sane. Dickens "has been popular chiefly because he was able to express in a comic, simplified, and therefore memorable form the native decency of the common man." Orwell, thinking of Dickens, sees in his mind's eye the face of a man who is "always fighting against something, but who fights in the open and is not frightened, the face of a man who is generously angry—in other words, of a nineteenth century liberal, a free intelligence, a type hated with equal hatred by all the smelly little orthodoxies which are now contending for our souls."

In 1939, in "Dickens: The Two Scrooges," Edmund Wilson also wrote appreciatively of the world's best-selling novelist, hoping to rescue him from his most visible admirers—all those "doddering Dickens fanciers" and "garrulous" memoir writers intent on preserving a sort of Santa Claus Dickens while writing books and articles "primarily interested in proving that Mr. Pickwick stopped at a certain inn and slept in a certain bed." Dickens, argued Wilson, was psychologically complex and artistically deep: it was absurd that "the Bloomsbury that talked about Dostoevsky ignored Dostoevsky's master, Dickens." Chesterton, wrote Wilson, had shown that Dickens "was incomparably the greatest English writer of his time; and Shaw coupled his name with Shakespeare. It is the conviction of the present writer that both these judgments were justified. Dickens—though he cannot of course pretend to the rank where Shakespeare has few companions—was nevertheless the greatest dramatic writer that the English had had since Shakespeare, and he created the largest and most varied world."

And who is to deny it? As a young man Dickens, in effect, stepped on a speeding train and never got off. The creator of Pickwick became the creator of Oliver Twist and David Copperfield and Pip. He became a generous host and a vivid public figure and the editor of a first-rate magazine and a key theatrical figure and, all things considered, the most influential social critic of the nineteenth century: the one writer whose depictions of greed and exploitation and poverty and urban suffering most directly shaped the moral imagination of his countrymen and—in so doing—not only helped crucially in making decades of measured political reforms possible, but in preserving, therefore, democratic ideals in Britain, its colonies, in Europe, and the United States.

Before his death Dickens often said that he wanted only to be remembered for his books and by his friends. Those friends are long gone, but as long as there are readers, Dickens' books will live on.

"It is one of my rules in life not to believe a man who may happen to tell you that he feels no interest in children. I hold myself bound to this principle by all kind consideration, because I know, as we all must, that any heart which would really toughen its affections and sympathies against those dear little people must be wanting in so many humanizing experiences of innocence and tenderness, as to be quite an unsafe monstrosity among men."

Charles Dickens, "Hospital for Sick Children,"
9 February 1858

Coffee For Thirty People.

Put 1 lb. of best coffee into a stewpan, sufficiently large to hold seven quarts of water; put it on the fire to dry the coffee (be sure to shake it, for fear it should burn); then take it off the fire and put the whites of two eggs into it, stir it till it is mixed, then pour on it six quarts of water, BOILING; let it stand a quarter of an hour, covered closely; then strain it through a jelly-bag, and put it away for use.

— from Catherine Dickens,
What Shall we Have for Dinner?

JOHN FORSTER ON DICKENS

❝ Of his attractive points in society and conversation I have particularised little, because in truth they were himself. Such as they were, they were never absent from him. His acute sense of enjoyment gave such relish to his social qualities that probably no man, not a great wit or a professed talker, ever left, in leaving any social gathering, a blank so impossible to fill up. In quick and varied sympathy, in ready adaptation to every whim or humour, in help to any mirth or game, he stood for a dozen men. If one may say such a thing, he seemed to be always the more himself for being somebody else, for continually putting off his personality. His versatility made him unique. What he said once of his own love of acting, applied to him equally when at his happiest among friends he loved; sketching a character, telling a story, acting a charade, taking part in a game; turning into comedy an incident of the day, describing the last good or bad thing he had seen, reproducing in quaint, tragical, or humorous form and figure, some part of the passionate life with which all his being overflowed. 'Assumption has charms for me so delightful—I hardly know for how many wild reasons—that I feel a loss of Oh I can't say what exquisite foolery, when I lose a chance of being someone not in the remotest degree like myself.' ❞

CAPSULE

SKETCHES BY BOZ.

1833-36

"What inexhaustible food for speculation do the streets of London afford!"

So begins one of the *Sketches By Boz*, the series of journalistic essays that Dickens wrote and published during the first years of his career. These pieces reveal much about his voice and style. They are playful, wry, and sometimes highly satiric. Their humor often derives from exaggeration, but at times they are very precisely descriptive, providing a vivid look at life in London in the 1830s. These *Sketches By Boz* derive from the young Dickens' fondness for roaming about and observing things and finding delight as well as pathos in the daily dramas of urban life.

In "Astley's," Boz describes a family—ma and pa and their "troop" of children dressed to the nines and taking their seats at Astley's Theatre, a process that generates plenty of fuss and bustle, and prompts the embarrassed eldest son, a teenager, to try "to look as if he did not belong to the family." When this self-conscious boy, who is "cultivating whiskers," is teased by his little brother, making ma and pa laugh, he assumes "a look of profound contempt, which lasted the whole evening."

Elsewhere Boz recalls the hassle of having to rise before dawn to catch an early coach; for "if there be one

thing in existence more miserable than another, it most unquestionably is the being compelled to rise by candlelight," particularly in the middle of February. You leave orders overnight to be "called at half-past four," but for most of the night you can only "doze for five minutes at the time, and start up suddenly from a terrific dream of a large church clock with the small hand running round, with astonishing rapidity, to every figure on the dial." But at last you drift into oblivion, and dream that you are "apprenticed to a trunk maker; how, or why, or when, or wherefore, you don't take the trouble to inquire; but there you are, pasting the lining in the lid of a portmanteau. Confound that other apprentice in the back shop, how he is hammering!—rap, rap, rap—what an industrious fellow he must be! You have heard him at work for half an hour past, and he has been hammering the incessantly the whole time. Rap, rap, rap, again—he's talking now—what's that he said? Five o'clock! You make a violent exertion, and start up in bed. The vision is at once dispelled; the trunk maker's shop is your own bedroom," and the other apprentice is actually the servant who, for half an hour, "has been vainly endeavoring to wake you," at "the imminent risk of breaking either his own knuckles or the panels of the door."

And then outside, rushing off without coffee, "you look down the long perspective of Oxford Street, the gaslights mournfully reflected on the wet pavement, and can discern no speck in the road to encourage the belief that there is a cab or a coach to be had—the very coachmen have gone home in despair." The cold sleet is drizzling down, and "the damp hangs upon the house tops and lamp posts and clings to you like an invisible cloak." But you trudge on, down Waterloo Place, on your way to the Golden Cross, where you learn that "the Birmingham High Flier" has not yet left, and you find yourself "feeling remarkably satisfied with yourself, and everything about you." By dawn the city starts to stir, and in the coach station "the early vendors of the morning papers have arrived, and you are assailed on all sides with shouts of '*Times*, gen'lm'n, *Times*,' 'Here's *Chron-Chron-Chron*,' '*Herald*, ma'am,' 'highly interesting murder, gen'llm'n,' 'Curious case o' breach o' promise, ladies.'"

His journalistic writings often show that Dickens had long enjoyed riding in omnibuses and trains, where the pleasures of motion and observation are uniquely combined—most of the time. "We once traveled four hundred miles, inside a stagecoach, with a stout man, who had a glass of rum and water, warm, handed in at the window at every place where we changed horses. This was decidedly unpleasant."

London, Boz shows, is full of quirky individuals; still, types abound. There are, for example, insolent cabmen and pompous clubmen and a great many "old boys" who pass their days in pubs with their papers and pipes and who tend to walk with "that grave, but confident, kind of roll, peculiar to old boys in general." And there are amusing groups of "London apprentices" who, on Sundays, like to stroll about the city's parks dressed in showy splendor with their patterned trousers and white kid gloves. Dickens gently mocks these young men, but he perhaps identifies with them too. They are vain, but not contemptible: "They are usually on the best terms with themselves, and it follows almost as a matter of course, in good humor with everyone about them."

But Boz, despite his own good humor, is also much drawn to scenes of sadness and decline. He visits a police office where a small crowd taunts a pair of young prostitutes, arrested and handcuffed together; he goes to Newgate Prison where he finds some "thirty prisoners, all under the sentence of death," including a burglar aged fourteen. He notes the wide presence of "shabby genteel" gentlemen who, once prosperous, now go about in suits without buttons and shiny with wear. He watches as shop after shop, in a city of shops, start up with hope and then struggle and fade a bit, and close. He visits a dreary pawnbroker's establishment in Drury Lane, "the door of which stands always doubtfully a little way open: half inviting, half-repelling the hesitating visitor who, if he be as yet un-initiated, examines one of the old garnet brooches in the window for a minute or two with affected eager-ness, as if he contemplated making a purchase: and then, looking cau-tiously round to ascertain that no one watches him, hastily slinks in."

From the start, Dickens was a po-litical writer, and some early sketches, like his early novels, contain homi-letic passages in which he denounces England's wide and easy toleration of poverty—the real source, in Dickens' view, of most crime. Another early piece, written under the pseudonym "Timothy Sparks," is "Sunday Un-der Three Heads," which attacks Sir Andrew Agnew's "Bill for the Bet-ter Observance of Sunday." This proposal would honor the Lord's Day by closing shops as well as all places of amusement as well. Dick-ens would always despise this strain of self-righteous Puritanism in Brit-ish society; Agnew's bill, he argues, was dehumanizing, and grossly un-fair, effecting neither the "pampered aristocrat, whose life is one contin-ued round of licentious pleasures and sensual gratifications," nor "the gloomy enthusiast, who detests the cheerful amusements he can never enjoy, and envies the healthy feelings he can never know, and who would put down the one and suppress the other, until he has made the minds of his fellow beings as besotted and distorted as his own." Who would suffer then? Only those "neat and clean, cheerful and contented" work-ing people, often hailed in Dickens'

fiction, for whom Sunday is likely to mean a picnic in the park or a day trip to Gravesend—a respite, in other words, from a week of hard labor.

Poverty, Dickens long held, was also mainly responsible for the wide-spread problem of alcoholism. "Gin drinking is a great vice in England," he writes in *Boz*, but "wretchedness and dirt are greater; and until you improve the homes of the poor, or persuade a half famished wretch not to seek re-lief in the temporary oblivion of his own misery, with the pittance which, divided among his family, would fur-nish a morsel of bread for each, gin shops will increase in number and splendour. If Temperance Societies would suggest an antidote against hunger, filth, and foul air, or could establish dispensaries for the gratu-itous distribution of bottles of Lethe water, gin palaces would be num-bered among the things that were."

Satire, sentiment, sharp obser-vation, social outrage, and time-less readability: the hallmarks of the Dickens method are all there in *Sketches By Boz*.

THE PICKWICK PAPERS.

1836-37

Dickens' first novel appeared in a series of 20 monthly parts; its action begins in the spring of 1827, when four members of a club devoted to amateur intellectual pursuits set forth on a sort of road trip to study human nature in a variety of forms.

The club's leader, Samuel Pickwick, is already much celebrated, at least among his fellow clubmen, for a paper intriguingly entitled "Speculations on the Source of the Hampstead Ponds, with Some Observations on the Theory of Tittlebats." On this journey the earnest Mr. Pickwick is joined by a trio of figures more suited for parts in a farce than for undertaking scientific research. Augustus Snodgrass is a lyrical soul "poetically enveloped" in a mysterious cloak. Nathaniel Winkle is a supposed sportsman who isn't quite certain how to fire a gun. And Tracy Tupman is a ladies' man who persists in his ardors even though "time and feeding had expanded" his "once romantic form."

Later, the group is joined by Sam Weller and his father Tony—a pair of streetwise Londoners whose language, rendered in Cockney dialect, provides the novel with much of its verve. Sam Weller, hired on as Pickwick's valet, has knocked around a bit; he knows first hand how the very poor live, those "worn-out, starving, houseless creeturs as rolls themselves in the dark corners o' them lonesome places" unable to afford a bed at two pence per night. But Weller is resilient and he has a taste for dark and ghoulish tales. Sam Weller has already studied human nature, from various angles; it's Sam Pickwick who still has much to learn.

Dickens, born in 1812, had been much influenced by the works of Fielding, Smollet, and Swift, and in many ways he continued to look at the world through eighteenth-century eyes. Dickens was not prudish, but he also recognized that the reading public had expanded and grown rather more censorious since the 1780s. Popular novels like *Tom Jones* (1749) and *Roderick Random* (1748) carried a certain air of decadence by the time Dickens began his writing career; they might be suitable for some mature men, but not for young people, certainly, or ladies of gentle breeding. Thus *Pickwick* offers up the spirited fun of Smollet's and Fielding's novels, but in a manner more akin to another of Dickens' favorite authors—Oliver Goldsmith. Like *The Vicar of Wakefield* (1766), which was hugely popular in its day, *The Pickwick Papers* is G-rated, suitable for general audiences. Or nearly suitable: surely some parts—including Sam Weller's tale of the man who invents a sausage-making machine and is ground to bits by his own invention—must have struck some parents as too ghoulish for children.

1836-37

The difference between *Pickwick* and *Roderick Random* can be detected in the way the two novels portray a similar comic situation. The story of a man who, in the dark of night, enters the wrong bed, intentionally or not, has almost certainly been around since human beings told funny stories, or had beds. Smollet's version, in *Roderick Random*, features a barber called Strap who mistakes one door for another and, in the darkness, slips into the bed of a man— Captain Weazel—who has momentarily gone off to void his bladder. When he returns, and finds Strap in his bed, the Captain "snatched up the vessel he had just filled, and emptied it at once on the astonished barber and his wife." As Strap protests ("I take God as a witness she's a virgin to me"), Mrs. Weazel throttles her husband with a shoe: "I'll teach you to empty your stink-pots on me."

There are no stinkpots about when Mr. Pickwick mistakenly enters the bed chamber of a "middle-aged lady in yellow curl papers" who is not all amused to find this portly, half-dressed man hovering about her bed. Throughout, Pickwick's integrity remains intact: he is distressed by "the very idea of exhibiting his night cap to a lady." Still, the lady in question angrily calls Pickwick "a wretch," and forces him to flee while clumsily gathering up his clothes as he goes. Pickwick, then, serves as a recurring figure in British comedy—the diffident male at the mercy of women far more commanding than himself.

In fact Mr. Pickwick, always well-intentioned, is unfailingly polite as well as naive, a real pigeon in a world replete with all sorts of predators and knaves and where words are barbed and tempers flare. After departing his small, orderly world of good cheer, Pickwick is, at various times, assaulted by a coach driver, assailed in a court trial, and imprisoned in a debtor's jail. *The Pickwick Papers* ends cheerfully, as Dickens' early novels do. But like *David Copperfield* and *Great Expectations*, *The Posthumous Papers of the Pickwick Club* is also very much about the bittersweet passage from innocence to experience that comes, inevitably, to us all.

Pickwick, as G. K. Chesterton writes, "is not a good novel." But "it is not a bad novel, for it is not a novel at all." He's right: in design, structure, and intent it's miles away from *Bleak House* and *Little Dorrit*. It's a prose romp, a fictional cabaret written quite on the fly, full of improvisations and interpolations, like "The Story of the Goblins Who Stole a Sexton," in which Gabriel Grub, a "surly" and "morose" grave keeper is, one Christmas Eve, beset by teasing Goblins. They cast a spell that compels the sexton to look at his "ill-humored" and malicious life, and at the struggles of others far more humble than himself. Grub "saw that men like himself, who snarled at the mirth and cheerfulness of others, were the foulest weeds on the fair surface of the earth." Ten years later, Grub becomes Scrooge as Dickens turns the tale into the more elaborate *A Christmas Carol*.

A Christian Writer

....

If we "remember the life and lessons of Our Lord Jesus Christ," Charles Dickens wrote, "and try to act up to them, we may confidently hope that God will forgive us our sins and mistakes, and enable us to live and die in Peace." More than twenty years later, Dickens asserted again: "I commit my soul to the mercy of God through our Lord and Saviour Jesus Christ."

Such direct statements of Christian belief are not often found among the major writers of Dickens' day. But then, Dickens' professions of faith also weren't meant for public display. They appear, respectively, in *The Life of Our Lord*, a book he wrote in 1846 for the private use of his children, and in his will, dated May 12, 1869. Many years later, one of those children, Henry Fielding Dickens, rightly noted that his father "never made a parade" of "his religious convictions." Nonetheless, those convictions were "very strong and deep."

Dickens' parents were nominal members of the Church of England, but while living in Chatham they also occasionally attended services at a nearby Baptist chapel. Though still a boy,

Dickens decided that he didn't like the "lumbering jocularity" of the chapel's preacher, recalling that he "regarded that reverend person in the light of a most dismal and oppressive charade." As an adult, Dickens attended both Anglican and Unitarian services. But he always preferred theatre-going to church-going.

It's not surprising, then, that Dickens named his sixth son after the author of *Joseph Andrews* and *Tom Jones*. Henry Fielding was one of Dickens great literary heroes—a satirical playwright and novelist who, as a practicing magistrate, was a part of, and not apart from, public life. Both Fielding and Dickens interpreted Christianity in a very broad-minded, very eighteenth-century way. They were much less interested in matters of dogma and ritual than in the moral imperatives of the New Testament. Both writers mocked religious hypocrites who, full of pride and hate, profess a faith of humility and love.

Dickens, then, had little interest in books about theology or religious history; he was, however, drawn to certain devotional and inspirational works, including Sydney Smith's sermons and Fielding's own *Journey from this World to the Next*. Dickens' religious readings suggest his belief in Providence, life after death and, most importantly, the Sermon on the Mount. This is how he ends *The Life of Our Lord*:

> Remember! – It is Christianity TO DO GOOD always—even to those who do evil to us. ... It is Christianity to be gentle, merciful, and forgiving, and ... to shew that we love Him by humbly trying to do right in everything. If we do this ... we may confidently hope that God will forgive us our sins and mistakes, and enable us to die in peace.

As his novels make plain, Dickens was not drawn to the concept of original sin and other beliefs that, in varying degrees, stressed the innate depravity of man. Such beliefs breed self-loathing and gloom, even among children who, in Dickens' rather romantic view, are likely to bloom more wholesomely when the stories they hear, and the images they see, are more hopeful and bright. And yet Dickens was a Protestant, through and through. Certainly his anti-Catholic prejudices were not at all unusual in the England of his day—just more colorfully expressed, especially in *Pictures from Italy*.

For Dickens, Italy was fluorescent in Catholic strangeness; and, in certain descriptions of Rome, his John Bull biases are on full display. He is much struck, for example, by the presence, seemingly everywhere, of monks, friars and priests. Of these, he is kindly to "the Cappuccini," who seem robust and forthright, acting as "the best friends of the people" and as true "counselors and comforters" to the distressed and the sick. But mainly Dickens sees the Catholic clergy as mere enforcers of an oppressive form of tyranny that holds sway by superstition and fear. Its most dreaded agents, the Jesuits, "muster strong in the streets, and go slinking noiselessly about, in pairs, like black cats."

The True Religion

He is shocked by the art that adorns churches everywhere all those images, obsessed with martyrdom, that present "grey-bearded men being boiled, fried, grilled, crimped, singed, eaten by wild beasts, worried by dogs, buried alive, torn asunder by horses, chopped up with small hatchets: women having their breasts torn with iron pinchers, their tongues cut out, their ears screwed off, their jaws broken, their bodies stretched upon the rack, or skinned upon the stake, or crackled up and melted in the fire"—"such a panorama of horror and butchery no man could imagine in his sleep, though he were to eat a whole pig raw, for supper."

One wonders, then, what Dickens had for supper when, in Genoa, he had a strange dream in which his dead sister-in-law, Mary Hogarth, appeared. She looked like one of Raphael's Madonnas—a loving spirit sent with a message from the other side. And so Dickens asked her: "What is the true religion?" When the spirit didn't reply, Dickens suggested, hopefully, that the outward expression of religion probably didn't matter as long as we always tried to "do good." But then he added, as if unconsciously aware that that the pageantry of Catholicism was not, in fact, alien to his own theatrical sensibility: "perhaps the Roman Catholic is the best?" "For you," the spirit promptly replied, "for you it is the best!"

Dickens had several Catholic friends, including the painter Stanfield Clarkson (who declined to illustrate *Pictures of Italy*.) and the writer Percy Fitzgerald, who was also "pained" by the "anti-Catholic" patches that would persist in Dickens' work. In *A Child's History of England* 1852, the Catholic Church is defined entirely as a political force forever menacing England and her allies. "When the massacre of Saint Bartholomew was yet fresh in their recollection," Dickens confidently reports, "a great Protestant Dutch hero, the Prince of Orange, was shot by an assassin who confessed that he had been kept and trained for the purpose in a college of Jesuits."

Accounts of Catholicism's strange excesses also turn up at times in *All the Year Round*; "Hysteria and Devotion" (1859) recalls the French nuns in Loudon who famously shocked ecclesiastical observers with unsettling displays of collective mania. *All the Year Round* keeps up the theme even after Dickens died and his son, Charles Jr., assumed the editor's chair. "Distortions of Christianity" (1870) decries the "blind obedience" St. Theresa supposedly demanded of her followers, and describes St. Francis of Assisi as a lunatic who, "for recreation," rolled "himself on thorns, went up to the neck in freezing ponds, and slept in the snow."

Thus the writer who believed in mesmerism and took a lively interest in the possible existence of ghosts had no patience for religious practices that were not Unitarian in spirit and manfully British in style. This he found, during his first visit to the United States, in a humble dockside chapel in Boston run by a former mariner—a "weather-beaten hard-featured man" whose countenance was nonetheless "pleasant and agreeable" and whose broadminded approach to Christian teaching stressed, in a charmingly gruff way, the message to do good always.

This was the sort of church that Ham and Mr. Peggotty might have attended, for the imagery in the preacher's sermon "was all drawn from the sea, and from the incidents of a seamen's life." Moreover, Dickens writes, the service was "plain and comprehensive in its doctrines, and breathed a tone of general sympathy and charity, which is not so commonly a characteristic of this form of address to the Deity as it might be."

CAPSULE

OLIVER TWIST.

1837-39

Oliver Twist started to appear as *Pick-wick* was starting to close. The novel's dark tone and grim urban setting surprised and bothered some readers, not least Lord Melbourne, the Prime Minister, who told Queen Victoria that he suspected that *Oliver Twist,* like John Gay's *A Beggar's Opera,* famously illustrated by William Hogarth, was not morally edifying. "I don't like that low debasing view of mankind," Melbourne asserted, according to the Queen's diaries. "I don't like those things. I wish to avoid them; I don't like them in reality, and therefore I don't wish to see them represented." *The London and Westminster Review* agreed. In *Oliver Twist,* "the accumulation of little details of misery and discomfort positively pains," complained the magazine, "and at last harasses the reader."

Dickens, in a later preface to the novel, admitted that most of its characters came from "the most criminal and degraded in London's population." But then, "I have yet to learn that a lesson of the purest good may not be drawn from the vilest evil. I saw no reason, when I wrote this book, why the very dregs of life, so long as their speech did not offend the ear, should not serve the purpose of a moral, at least as well as its froth and cream. Nor did I doubt that there lay festering in St. Giles's, as good materials towards the truth as any to be found in St. James's." Moreover, he stressed, the world is quite full of such men as Bill Sikes, the thief and murderer who is quite without pity or remorse, and in whom "every gentler human feeling is dead." *Oliver Twist,* wrote its author, shows something of "the best and worst shades of our nature; much of its ugliest hues, and something of its most beautiful."

Oliver himself, like Ebenezer Scrooge, is recognized around the world, even by those who have never read a word of Dickens' prose. Like *A Christmas Carol,* the novel has been repeatedly dramatized for the stage, television, and film; its striking characters have appeared in countless cartoons, comic books, and radio plays. Oliver, everybody knows, is a half-starved workhouse orphan who is punished when he begs his keepers for a bit more gruel. He wanders the streets, sleeps rough, and is finally given a home by kind and generous people—but not before he is lured into the horrid den of Fagin, a dealer in stolen goods who also schools young boys in the rules and practices of a successful life in crime.

Oliver is not the novel's most compelling figure: he's "a mere child" who, through no fault of his own, begins life at the mercy of adults far crueler and better fed than himself; and who, in this hard environment, would necessarily develop his own brutish tendencies in order to survive. Dickens, who had walked all over London's streets as a boy and later as a young reporter, notes that he had seen countless young men in similar circumstances, scrapping on the margins as petty criminals or barely paid factory hands. In *The Real Oliver Twist* (2005), Robert Walder suggests that Dickens may also have been inspired, at least in part, by *The Memoirs of Robert Blincoe*, which appeared in 1828 in *The Lion*, a radical newspaper, and then four years later in book form.

Blincoe was also an orphan who began working as a child in dangerous jobs. Some of his mates, he records, started work at the age of six as chimney sweeps—a job Oliver particularly fears given the notoriously high rate of sickness and death among boys forced to toil long hours in the thick of soot and grime. Blincoe himself worked in a factory where he once witnessed the death of a co-worker, a girl of ten, who was crushed when her apron was caught up in a powerful machine. Her blood, recalled Blincoe, was "thrown about like water from a twirled mop." Blincoe survived his trials and later owned a successful business; his memoir, like *Oliver Twist*, played its own part in helping improve labor conditions for children, particularly in the textile industry.

Fagin also had a real-life counterpart: Ikey Solomon, a London forger and thief whose career was tracked, sensationally, in popular publications of the day. (Thackeray even used "Ikey Solomon, Esq., junior" as a figure in his fiction.) Solomon, a prodigy of bad behavior, formed pickpocket rings at the age of fourteen, and later ran a thriving racket dealing in prostitution and stolen goods. Like Fagin, Solomon was eventually jailed, but he escaped execution and—like Wilkins Micawber and Abel Magwitch—he tried to start over in Australia. However, the so-called "Prince of the Fences" found neither lasting wealth nor respectability as an immigrant to the colonies, and he died broke in Tasmania in the 1850s.

From the start, readers of *Oliver Twist* were troubled by the novel's frequent reference to Fagin as "the Jew"—as if his criminality and ethnic identity were somehow one in the same. Certainly, a casual anti-Semiticism was simply part of the cultural atmosphere in Dickens' day, evidenced (for example) in the constant and at times vicious public attacks that Benjamin Disraeli faced throughout his career. And both Thackeray and Anthony Trollope, among others, left anti-Semitic touches in their work.

Dickens, alas, carried his own religious and racial prejudices, but these were comparatively mild and tempered by a real proclivity toward the sort of cosmopolitanism that he admired in his eighteenth-century literary heroes, and that he aimed to project in both *Household Words* and *All the Year Round*. Dickens, moreover, regretted offending many Jewish readers with Fagin's portrayal, and he tried to make amends with his more sympathetic portrait of the venerable Riah in *Our Mutual Friend*. In *A Child's History of England* (1852), moreover, Dickens is careful to note that Jews in England had long been treated "heartlessly" and "suffered so much." During the reign of Edward I, Dickens writes, members of the Jewish

1837-39

population "were most unmercifully pillaged," heavily taxed, and "taken up with their wives and children and thrown into beastly prisons, until they purchased their release by paying to the king twelve thousand pounds."

Like Dickens' other early novels and stories, *Oliver Twist* became a cultural phenomenon, prompting not only wide press commentary, but assorted product tie ins (dolls and figurines were popular) and numerous stage productions of varying quality. In one of his memoirs George Sala recalls witnessing, at the Old Adelphi Theatre, the authorized production, on the same night, of *Twist* and *Nicholas Nickleby*, featuring some of London's leading actors. "There will never be effaced from my mind's eye," writes Sala, "the image of Frederick Yates as Fagin frying sausages in the thieves' den, a room hung all around with clothes-lines supporting stolen pocket handkerchiefs; of Mrs. Keeley, both as Oliver and Smike; and of that most powerful melodramatic actor, O. Smith, as Bill Sikes."

Writing in the *Literary Gazette,* an anonymous reviewer of *Oliver Twist* also called attention to the Adelphi production, and noted how the audience, consisting of "all classes," responded so readily to each of the characters as they appeared. Dickens' characterizations, suggested the reviewer, had already won him "true fame." Walter Scott, he noted, had created a large cast of well-known characters, including Meg Merrilies, Dominie Sampson, and Rob Roy. But among other names "celebrated in our literature, we find that the creation of a single character, or of two, three, or four, has been deemed sufficient to exalt the reputation of a writer. Robinson Crusoe and Friday glorify the name of De Foe; Uncle Toby and Corporal Trim, Mr Shandy and Dr. Slop, are enough for Sterne; John Gilpin, for Cowper; Tam O'Shanter and his comrades, for Burns; and we might enumerate a hundred similar instances. Then look at Dickens—a young man, and not above two or three years before the public. Already has he peopled the regions of imagination with a crowd of new creatures. It would require a page to record them, from Pickwick and Weller to Squeers, Ralph Nickleby, Smike and Newman Noggs— all very original, and all true to the life. At the close of a long career, Richardson, Fielding, Smollett, our brightest lights in fiction, had done no more than he has achieved within this wonderfully short space."

Dickens, moreover, has "dug deep into the human mind; and he has nobly directed his energies to the exposure of evils—the workhouse, the starving school, the factory system, and many other things, at which blessed nature shudders and recoils. As a moralist and reformer of cruel abuses, we have the warmer thanks of the community to offer him. ...."

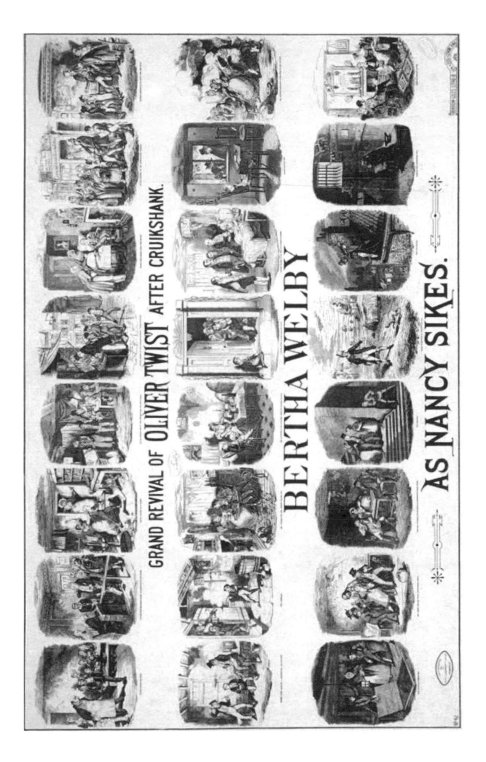

GRAND REVIVAL OF OLIVER TWIST AFTER CRUIKSHANK.

BERTHA WELBY

AS NANCY SIKES.

NICHOLAS NICKLEBY.

1838-39

Nicholas Nickleby follows the fortunes of an "open, handsome, and ingenuous" young man who, after his father's death, takes up the support of his mother and his sister, Kate. Early on Nicholas' uncle, Ralph Nickleby, appears ready to assist the fatherless family. But Ralph, a dodgy businessman ("the old sinner," the novel calls him), is better at inflicting harm than offering help. And he's so morbid that he's happy to see himself as "not a man to be moved by a pretty face. There is a grinning skull beneath it, and men like me who look and work below the surface see that, and not its delicate covering."

Dickens' early novels are particularly blunt in the way they divide the world between the mentally healthy and the mentally sick—between generous, light-hearted souls on the one hand, and cruel, life-denying misers like Ralph Nickleby and Wackford Squeers on the other.

Squeers, one of Dickens' great villains, runs Dotheboys Hall, the grim boarding school where Nicholas, at his uncle's urging, takes a job. Squeers is an ignorant lout, and Dotheboys Hall is little more than a prison camp where orphaned or abandoned boys are left uneducated and unfed. Nicholas is so innocent that he accepts the job with grati-tude: Squeers, he concedes, "is an odd-looking man, but what of that? Porson was an odd-looking man, and so was Doctor Johnson; all these bookworms are."

Dotheboys Hall was based on a real school, the Bowes Academy in Durham. In 1823, the school's headmaster, William Shaw, had been charged with negligence after several students went blind. Like Squeers, Shaw wore an eye patch, and he became, after the Bowes scandal, a figure of scorn. Some recent research, however, suggests that Shaw, far from being Squeers-like, was a decent educator respected by his pupils. And the blindness at Bowes was very possibly caused not by the maintenance of poor diets, but by an outbreak of trachoma that Shaw tried earnestly to treat. Dickens, who met Shaw, thus sullied his memory, say some, by turning him into the tyrannical Squeers.

Dickens, though, wasn't working as an objective reporter when he wrote *Nickleby*—or any of his other novels. He was always, above all else, a comic writer with a satirical streak and a high talent for parody and exaggeration. For Dickens, Squeers represents the larger reality that many English schools—including the one Dickens himself attended—were run by cruel men who hadn't a clue.

1838-39

William Squeers probably owes as much to William Jones, headmaster of the Wellington House Academy, as he does to William Shaw.

In *Nickleby*, satire and melodrama sit happily side by side. The novel features several stagy, villainous characters and theatrical scenes. Kate, pushed into the world, finds herself pursued by Sir Mulberry Hawk—for Dickens a particularly loathsome example of the aristocratic class. There's no subtlety in Dickens' portrait of Hawk: he's a "fashionable vagabond," and the gaze he directs at Kate is "odious," "insolent," and "repulsive." But the poor girl ("who had done no wrong save that of coming into the world alive") is no pushover, and she rebuffs Hawk in decisive terms: "Unhand me, sir!"

Nicholas Nickleby (which is dedicated to the actor William Macready) both praises and parodies the popular theatre of its day. Nicholas, after leaving Dotheboys Hall, finds himself in an acting company led by Vincent Crummles, a self-promoting eccentric who casts members of his family, including Miss Ninetta Crummles—the ageless "Infant Phenomenon"—in an eclectic repertoire that ranges from *Macbeth* to something called *The Fairy Porcupine*. Crummles is something of a scamp, but he belongs to what is, in Dickens, a not ignoble fraternity of actors, entertainers, impresarios, and others who recognize that imaginative entertainment and spirited diversion are an essential part of human life. Dickens salutes Crummles'

generosity and pluck, his willingness to put on an elaborate wig of some sort and assume a variety of flamboyant roles.

Dickens hated—even more than bad acting—the unauthorized use of his work in print or on stage. In *Nicholas Nickleby* he finds space to attack literary piracy—as he would even more vehemently during his first American tour in 1842. Here, he allows Nicholas to confront a certain "literary gentleman" who, with others of his ilk, routinely "take the uncompleted books of living authors, fresh from their hands, wet from the press, cut, hack, and carve them" for purposes of their own; who indeed also publish, in "mean pamphlets," under their own names, "garbled extracts" from other, more accomplished authors, including, say, Charles Dickens.

"Now," asserts Nicholas, using words that Dickens in America would often repeat, "show me how the distinction between such pilfering as this, and picking a man's pocket in the street: unless, indeed, it be that the legislature has a regard for pocket-handkerchiefs, and leaves men's brains, except when they are knocked out by violence, to take care of themselves."

THE OLD CURIOSITY SHOP.

1840-41

It's not possible to picture, say, E.M. Forster ever writing a book remotely like *The Old Curiosity Shop*. But one can more plausibly suggest that if Monty Python, Ferderico Fellini, and Walt Disney had ever collaborated artistically, they might well have produced something very similar, in subject and tone, to Dickens' 1841 novel, where the comic and the macabre, the sentimental and the surreal, are all strikingly combined.

In *The Old Curiosity Shop* the faultless Little Nell Trent runs, with her grandfather, a gambling addict, from the beastly Daniel Quilp. It's full of odd and menacing and cartoonish characters, like the shady attorney Sampson Brass, a "tall, meager man, with a nose like a wen," whose "blandest smiles" are "extremely forbidding." Sally Brass, his bony sister, sports on her head a brown gauze scarf which, like "the wing of the fabled vampire," could be "twisted into any form that happened to suggest itself."

There are itinerant showmen like Vuffin who manages a "giant," a "little lady without legs or arms" and a "silent gentleman" who "had rather deranged the natural expression of his countenance by putting small leaden lozenges into his eyes and bringing them out at his mouth." The distinctive Mrs. Jarley, meanwhile, operates a travelling exhibition in which "pigeon-breasted" wax figures, "very blue about the beards," all stand "looking intensely nowhere, and staring with extraordinary care at nothing."

Moreover, there is Richard Swiveller—a young version of the sort of florid, self-inventing figure that would always attract Dickens' interest. Dick Swiveller is a shabby clerk who fancies himself a bit of a gentleman and so, with mingled results, he cultivates a certain style. A mix of raffishness and charm (Quilp hails his "great expectations"), Swiveller is an early sketch for both William Dorrit and Wilkins Micawber. "And say," Swiveller tells Quilp, "say, sir, that I wafted here upon the pinions of concord; that I came to remove, with the rake of friendship, the seeds of mutual violence and heart-burning, and so to sow in their place, the germs of social harmony."

And there is Mrs. Wackles, who runs a girls' school, "an excellent, but rather venomous lady of three score." Miss Monflathers, a teacher at the school and a model of self-congratulation, denounces Nell for working at Mrs. Jellyby's wax works, and is pleased to think that her "home-thrust" had "hit very hard."

But then, nearly everyone cuffs Little Nell around, one way or another. She is imposed upon by her kindly old grandfather; considered a commodity of sorts by her younger brother; and—it's strongly implied—is lusted after by more than one

1840-41

low-rent roué. It's not easy being a pretty, good-hearted thirteen-year-old in such a cold and difficult world.

Daniel Quilp badly wants Little Nell. Quilp lends money, collects rent, abuses his wife, and heckles his mother-in-law. "I don't eat babies," he clarifies, "I don't like 'em." But he does eat "hard eggs, shell and all," and "gigantic prawns with the heads and tails on." He drinks boiling tea "without winking." He is "so low in stature as to be quite a dwarf, though his head and face were large enough for the body of a giant." He's "crafty," malicious, and full of restless energy—a fairy tale monster, the unrestrained Id. He's a "perpetual nightmare" to Little Nell, and he dogs her with demonic glee.

Much of the book's imagery underscores its dark, nightmarish tone. In a dull town, on a sunny day, Dickens notes that "the very dogs were all asleep, and the flies, drunk with moist sugar in the grocer's shop, forgot their wings and briskness, and baked to death in dusty corners of the window." Elsewhere, "some summer insect, with no escape into the air, flew blindly to and fro, beating its body against the walls and ceiling, and filling the silent place with murmurs."

Cruelty, caprice, sadness, suffering: such things are plentiful in *The Old Curiosity Shop*. Nell and her grandfather wander far from home, "alone in the world," looking for the "peace of mind and happiness they once enjoyed." Nell dies, but not before she witnesses the demise of another child, "The Little Scholar." Life is a losing battle, full of vile predators and vulnerable prey. No wonder Mr. Codlin considers himself "doomed to contemplate the harsh realities of existence."

But this is Dickens, after all, not Nathaniel West. And the world he portrays is multivarious, full of light and dark, good and bad. The world itself is The Old Curiosity Shop, where amid the grim jumble of cruelty and want there is much that glimmers and shines. Kit Nubbles, the boy who admires Nell and seeks to protect her, finds much delight in life. His family is good natured, kind, and content. In one scene we casually find Kit's baby brother, "sitting up in his mother's lap," while "trying to force a large orange into his mouth, and gazing intently at the lights in the chandelier."

According to John Forster, the Garlands had real-life models. Dickens told him that, when he was a boy working in London, he lodged with a protective family that took heed of the sharp abdominal pains he sometimes felt (throughout his life, in fact) during times of stress. Mr. Garland "was lame, and had a quiet old wife; and he had a very innocent grown-up son, who was lame, too. They were all very kind to the boy. He was taken with one of his old attacks of spasm one night, and the whole three of them were about his bed until morning. They were all dead when he told me this, but in another form they still live very pleasantly as the Garland family in *The Old Curiosity Shop*."

Dickens and Animals

....

In his *Memories of My Father,* Dickens' sixth son, Henry Fielding, noted that "I had an extraordinary letter only a short time ago in which I was seriously asked if it were true that my father had an objection to all animals except horses."

It was "preposterous question," Henry declared. "Nothing could be further from the truth. He loved all domestic animals," particularly dogs. These included Turk, a "sweet-tempered mastiff," and Linda, a St. Bernard, who often romped beside him in the Kentish countryside. Thus Henry would recall "with the utmost vividness the long walks in the afternoon when his desk work was done, ten miles or more, when I and the dogs were sometimes his sole companions. He rarely went out without his dogs, and I remember the villagers used to talk about Mr. Dickens with his *roost* of dogs, a quaint expression in that connection."

Dickens also kept birds including, earlier in his career, ravens. In 1850 Dickens published three essays under the title "From the Raven in the Happy Family." The narrating raven is a perceptive and acerbic fellow eager to let his human readers know that the animals around them are not, in their secret lives, much impressed.

Dickens' raven casts a cold eye on the human menagerie, mocking many of the same pretensions and follies that aroused the scorn of Dickens himself.

Dickens' raven is on conversational terms with many animals including "my honourable friend, the dog—I call him my honourable friend in your Parliamentary sense, because I hate him. He "turns round three times before he goes to sleep. I ask him why? He says he don't know; but he always does it."

Dogs may be generally content with their lot, but horses, the raven reports, are not. Daily they take great abuse from "you Lords of the Creation, as you call yourselves." Man, according to the Horse, is "very unintelligible in his caprices; seldom expressing with distinctness what he wants of us; and relying greatly on our better judgment to find out. He is cruel and fond of blood— particularly at a steeple-chase—and is very ungrateful."

The Raven particularly mocks Man's endless compulsion to be "genteel." Consider funerals. "Don't I know a Raven in a Cathedral town," he croaks, "who has often heard your service for the Dead?" The two birds agree: it's a "nonsensical mockery," these expensive rituals, with their hired mourners, flowing black scarves, and huge coaches pulled by horses adorned with feathers—services that, ironically, always begin with the words "'We brought nothing into this world, and it is certain that we can carry nothing out.'"

"You who are not poor," asserts Dickens' raven, "ought to set 'em an example," because "besides making the whole thing costly, you've confused their minds about this business, and have taught 'em to confound expense and show, with respect and affection."

Birds of a Feather

Dickens was most fond of a particular pet raven, Grip, whose habits and remarks he often recorded with amusement in letters to friends. One of Dickens' acquaintances, James T. Fields, would recall the novelist's liking for birds, often made obvious as the two men walked in the fields and lanes around Gad's Hill. Dickens' gifts of mimicry extended to animals as well as people, as Field relates; he was "quite a fund of canary-bird anecdotes, and the pert ways of birds that picked up worms for a living afforded him infinite amusement. He would give a capital imitation of the way a robin-redbreast cocks his head on one side preliminary to a dash forward in the direction of a wriggling victim. There is a small grave at Gad's Hill to which Dickens would occasionally take a friend, and it was a privilege to stand with him be-side the burial-place of little Dick, the family's favorite canary."

Animals appear frequently and sympathetically in Dickens' fiction, often with amusing human traits: think only of the fictional Grip, Barnaby Rudge's raven, who moves not in "a hop, or walk, or run, but in a pace like that of a very particular gentleman with exceedingly tight boots on, trying to walk fast over loose pebbles."

Dickens was also respectfully fond of cats, despite their native dislike of birds. In Dickens' writing, cats tend to be sly, "rakish-looking," and a bit hedonistic: "Watch a cat in a field or garden, on a bright sunny day—how she crouches in the mould, rolls in the sand, basks in the grass, delights to vary the surface upon which she rests, and changes the form of the substance upon which she takes her ease." In *Dombey and Son* Mrs Pipchin "had an old black cat, who generally lay coiled upon the centre foot of the fender, purring egotistically, and winking at the fire until the contracted pupils of his eyes were like two notes of admiration."

Dogs, by contrast, display a clumsy confidence, a blunt sincerity; they are contemplative in their cryptic canine way. "I know a shaggy black and white dog," Dickens relates in an 1860 essay, "who keeps a drover. He is a dog of an easy disposition, and too frequently allows his drover to get drunk. On these occasions, it is the dog's custom to sit outside the public house, keeping his eye on a few sheep, and thinking. I have seen him with six sheep, plainly casting up in his mind how many he began with when he left the market, and at what places he left the rest. ..."

Beasts of Burden

Moreover Dickens notably denounced cruelty to animals, sometimes in the pages of *Household Words*. In 1850 the magazine exposed the brutal practices at London's Smithfield Cattle Market, where sheep and cattle raised carefully on country farms were brought to be weighed, priced, and sold for slaughter.

In "The Heart of Mid-London" (1850), Dickens and his co-author, W.H. Wills, expose the inhumanity that prevailed at the Smithfield Market. They describe the savage glee of the many club-wielding men who drove and harried these beasts, refusing them food and forcing them into over-crowded pens. Ironically, the Market—where animals were, in effect, tortured before they were killed—stood close to the gate of St. Bartholomew's Hospital. To reflect, Dickens wrote, that the gate of this great hospital was in the midst of this devilry, and that such a monument of years of sympathy for human pain should stand there, jostling this disgraceful record of years of disregard of brute endurance—to look up at the faint lights in the windows of the houses where the people were asleep, and to think that some of them had been to public prayers that Sunday, and had typified the Divine love and gentleness, by the panting, footsore creature, burnt, beaten, and needlessly tormented there, that night, by thousands—suggested truths so inconsistent and so shocking, that the Market of the Capital of the World seemed a ghastly and blasphemous Nightmare.

Apparently Dickens had once heard, from Thackeray, that Italians were kinder to animals all-around. But Dickens was not convinced: man's inhumanity to animals was, he discerned, a common state. In *Pictures from Italy* Dickens describes with disgust how oxen used in the excavation of marble were still made to carry and haul great weights up and down steep hills and were still "worn to death" by their exertions. They are beaten by a man—"the very Devil of true despotism"—who uses a great rod with an iron point to keep the beasts going, poking it into their bodies, beating it on their heads, even screwing "it round and round in their nostrils." The despot gives a "great whoop and hallo" when the beasts complete their tasks, although Dickens notes that he seems quite oblivious to the fact that someday they might "shake him off, and blindly mash his brains upon the road, in the noontide of his triumph."

For Dickens the episode illustrates the brute inequities of society and the cruel hardness of life. Human beings and animals are united by suffering. After watching the oxen and their drivers dig and haul and struggle he finds himself standing "in one of the many studii of Carrara," a great workshop "full of beautifully-finished copies in marble, of almost every figure, group, and bust." It "seemed, at first, so strange to me that those exquisite shapes, replete with grace, and thought, and delicate repose, should grow out of all this toil, and sweat, and torture!"

But "I soon found a parallel to it," he decides, "an explanation of it, in every virtue that springs up in miserable ground, and every good thing that has its birth in sorrow and distress. And looking out of the sculptor's great window, upon the marble mountains, all red and glowing in the decline of day, but stern and solemn to the last, I thought, my God! how many quarries of human hearts and souls, capable of far more beautiful results, are left shut up and mouldering away: while pleasure-travelers through life, avert their faces as they pass, and shudder at the gloom and ruggedness that conceal them!"

DICKENS ON VICE AND CRIME

❝ It is to be observed, that those who are most distrustful of the advantages of education, are always the first to exclaim against the results of ignorance. This fact was pleasantly illustrated on the railway, as I came here. In the same carriage with me there sat an ancient gentleman (I feel no delicacy in alluding to him, for I know that he is not in the room, having got out far short of Birmingham), who expressed himself most mournfully as to the ruinous effects and rapid spread of railways, and was most pathetic upon the virtues of the slow-going old stage coaches. Now I, entertaining some little lingering kindness for the road, made shift to express my concurrence with the old gentleman's opinion, without any great compromise of principle. Well, we got on tolerably comfortably together, and when the engine, with a frightful screech, dived into some dark abyss, like some strange aquatic monster, the old gentleman said it would never do, and I agreed with him. When it parted from each successive station, with a shock and a shriek as if it had had a double-tooth drawn, the old gentleman shook his head, and I shook mine. When he burst forth against such new-fangled notions, and said no good could come of them, I did not contest the point. But I found that when the speed of the engine was abated, or there was a prolonged stay at any station, up the old gentleman was at arms, and his watch was instantly out of his pocket, denouncing the slowness of our progress. Now I could not help comparing this old gentleman to that ingenious class of persons who are in the constant habit of declaiming against the vices and crimes of society, and at the same time are the first and foremost to assert that vice and crime have not their common origin in ignorance and discontent. ❞

—Charles Dickens, speaking in support of the Birmingham Polytechnic Institution, February 28, 1844.

CAPSULE

BARNABY RUDGE.

1843-44

This curious and relatively little-read title was Dickens' fifth novel; it was supposed to be his first. He had conceived of it even before he began writing *The Pickwick Papers*. But when *Pickwick* took off, Dickens put *Barnaby Rudge* aside. From the start, he wanted to write an historical novel with the locksmith Gabriel Varden as its central character. Varden is a "round, red-faced sturdy yeoman, with a double-chin, and a voice husky with good living, good sleeping, good humour, and good health." He is "bluff, hale, hearty"— a decent, likable man, not entirely unlike Samuel Pickwick, who finds himself living in turbulent times.

Varden heads a colorful family. His daughter Dolly has a "roguish face"—the face of "a pretty, laughing, girl; dimpled and fresh, and healthful—the very impersonation of good-humour and blooming beauty." His "plump and buxom" wife has "what is commonly called an uncertain temper—a phrase which being interpreted signifies a temper tolerably certain to make everybody more or less uncomfortable. Thus it generally happened, that when other people were merry, Mrs. Varden was dull; and that when other people were dull, Mrs. Varden was disposed to be amazingly cheerful."

The Vardens, though, do not dominate the work, which opens in 1775 and culminates in the "No Popery Riots" led by Lord George Gordon in the summer of 1780. The riots were a reaction, more or less, to the Papists Act of 1778 which sought to lift a series of restrictions long placed on Roman Catholics in the United Kingdom. Gordon sought repeal of the measure, forming a Protestant Association to further his cause. Gordon, born into Scottish nobility, was an eccentric, if unstable character who eventually wound up serving a long stretch in prison, where he converted to Judaism. Dickens notes the "gravity of his dress" and his "stiffness of deportment." He "wore an air of melancholy; but it was suggestive of an air of indefinable uneasiness, which infected those who looked upon him, and filled them with a kind of pity for the man: though why it did so, they would have some trouble to explain."

From the start of his career, Dickens had worried about an explosion of civil unrest in Britain; in fact much of his journalism is fueled by the tacit assumption that, if Britain's democratic institutions remained largely stagnant and corrupt, the county would face its own bloody revolution—a deeply frightening prospect for a man who had worked hard to enter the middle class and who was constitutionally drawn to the idea of order in all things. For Dickens, Gordon was frightening not because he was a fanatic anti-Catholic, but because he was highly effective in rousing a mob.

Gordon had a nature "prone to false enthusiasm, and the vanity of being a leader." All the rest, Dickens writes, "was weakness—sheer weakness; and it is the unhappy lot of thoroughly weak men, that their very sympathies, affections, confidences—all the qualities which in better constituted minds are virtues—dwindle into foibles, or turn into downright weaknesses."

There are two Barnaby Rudges, it turns out. The elder Rudge is an accused criminal and a fugitive who drifts in and out of the novel's action. The younger Barnaby Rudge is more interesting, a long-haired, simple-minded young man who wears motley clothes, keeps a very sharp-minded raven, and who gets caught up in Gordon's great riot and finds himself sentenced to death. Barnaby is saved, with Gabriel Varden's help; but Dickens manages—in the novel's concluding chapters—to convey well the horrors of public executions, as he would once again, more famously, in his second and far better historical novel, *A Tale of Two Cities.*

Damn Yankees

....

In January 1842, Charles Dickens boarded a large steamship and sailed to North America for the first time. He was accompanied by his wife, Catherine, his wife's maid, Anne Brown, and a literary reputation big enough for a dozen men. At 30, Dickens was as famous as Byron. He was more popular than Oliver Goldsmith, and often hailed as the next Walter Scott. At least one American admirer assured him that his trip there would "be such a triumph from one end of the States to the other, as was never known in any nation."

But six months later, his American tour nearly complete, Dickens could barely wait to board the ship for home. He missed his children, of course, his large circle of friends, and the daily routines that structured his writing life. But he was also deeply weary of all things American, and the longer he stayed in the United States the less he found to admire and like. Many Americans, moreover, were happy to see Dickens go. The Great Boz, wrote one editorialist, was "no gentleman" but "a mere mercenary scoundrel."

What happened?

There was, for starters, an unfortunate ocean crossing. As he records in *American Notes* (1842), Dickens had been assured by the Britannia steam-packet company that sailing in the dead of winter presented no special challenges. In fact, on a previous January crossing, nobody was ill and everybody danced from morning till night: it was "a piece of the purest frolic, and delight, and

jollity!" Moreover Dickens had been promised spacious accommodations.

Instead he found himself in a "preposterous box" which was no more likely to hold his luggage than "a giraffe could be persuaded or forced into a flower-pot." And the sea was so rough that Dickens became sea-sick—"not sea-sick, be it understood, in the ordinary acceptation of the term." "I lay there, all the day long, quite coolly and contentedly, with no sense of weariness, with no desire to get up, or get better, or take the air; with no curiosity, or care." If "Neptune himself had walked in, with a toasted shark on his trident, I should have looked upon the event as one of the very commonest everyday occurrences."

Once, despite the "heavy sea" and the crushing "head-wind" Dickens found himself on deck. "I found myself standing, when a gleam of consciousness came upon me, holding on to something. I don't know what. I think it was the boatswain: or it may have been the pump: or possibly the cow." "I could not even make out which was the sea," he continues, "and which the sky, for the horizon seemed drunk, and was flying wildly about in all directions." Once, after a roaring storm, he noticed that the life-boat "had been crushed by one blow of the sea like a walnut-shell; and there it hung dangling in the air: a mere faggot of crazy boards."

But finally, after arriving on Boston, Dickens was disposed to be impressed. Previous books about America by British travelers—including Fanny Trollope and Captain Marryat—had not been flattering. Dickens, however, found many things to his liking, including the artless hospitality of many natives, and the fact that some public institutions, like the Massachusetts Asylum for the Blind, stood in "cheerful healthy" locations, and were places where "good order" and "cleanliness" prevailed.

The charm wore off, however, and Dickens felt increasingly put upon, crowded and, at least in the case of copyright law, deeply wronged. Everywhere he was saluted, honored, feted; everywhere someone wanted to shake his hand or take a clipping of his hair. He'd become an odd specimen, he thought, and nothing bothered him more than being stared at, through windows, by strangers, even as he washed his face or took a nap. In England, to be sure, assorted admirers and beggars were quite willing to chase him down in the hope of a favor or a spare shilling. But it was nothing like this.

A Tempest of Spitting

The Americans and English, Dickens discerned, differed on other key points of etiquette—not least in their attitudes toward public spitting. The Yanks, Dickens decided, were very much for it; throughout *American Notes* the spit flies, along with tobacco juice, phlegm, and whatever else could be expectorated in a loud and dramatic way, and often with scant regard for where, exactly, it might land. In one letter Dickens recalls sleeping on a canal boat, in a low berth, in tight quarters. All night the men above and beside him spat so copiously that "there was a perfect storm and tempest of spitting." Dickens' coat, unfortunately, was "in the very centre of the hurricane," and so "I was fain the next morning to lay it on the deck, and rub it down with fair water before it was in a condition to be worn again."

A certain casualness regarding personal hygiene and personal space was—as Dickens discovered—a recurring American trait. In *American Notes* he describes, for example, the woman who was "an upper domestic" in the Ohio boarding establishment where he was staying, "and who, when she came to wait upon us at any meal, sat herself down comfortably in the most convenient chair, and producing a large pin to pick her teeth with, remained performing that ceremony, and steadfastly regarding us meanwhile with as much gravity and composure (now and then pressing us to eat a little more), until it was time to clear away."

But clearly nothing bothered Dickens more than the fact that so many American book and newspaper publishers made unauthorized use of his works, often cutting here and revising there to better meet "American tastes." Many prominent American authors and journalists supported the campaign for a copyright law that would be strictly enforced in both Europe and the United States. But Dickens, it seems, took every opportunity to press his case. Thus, speaking in Hartford, he noted that the great Sir Walter Scott himself, similarly robbed of royalties, had died under a heavy burden of debt. "My blood so boiled as I thought of the monstrous injustice," Dickens told Forster, that "I felt as if I were twelve feet high when I thrust it down their throats."

Some Americans, however, objected to the hard sell. And they found Dickens objectionable in other ways. He had, after all, declined President John Tyler's invitation to a White House dinner, and had rushed through lunch with ex-president John Quincy Adams. According to one observer, Dickens "seemed rather to prefer dining with reporters and newspaper men than with persons in official position"—just as he did back home.

Dickens' youth and manner also bothered some of his American hosts; apparently, they had expected a more mature and sedate literary figure. "He wears entirely too much jewelry," noted one member of Tyler's family. His hair, observed the writer Richard Henry Dana, was "matted, curling, wet-looking," and nearly as objectionable as his "dissipated looking mouth" and his "muddy olive complexion" and "stubby fingers & hands by no means patrician." Dana was attracted to

Dickens' "hearty, off-hand manner" and his "dashing way of talking." "There is a fascination about him which keeps your eyes on him, yet you cannot get over the impression that he is a low-bred man." "Take the genius out of his face," suggested Dana, the son of a prominent Boston author, and "there are a thousand young London shop-keepers" who "look exactly like him."

Not surprisingly, the "low-bred" man who wrote *Oliver Twist* took notice of the defeated and the poor. He was disgusted by slavery's brutalizing reality; by the fatuous and pompous arguments he heard in its defense; by the pitiable sight of men and women marked by the lash; by the sense of "decay and gloom" that hovered over Richmond and other places where the spirit of slavery prevailed. Elsewhere, a small band of bedraggled indians, "riding on shaggy ponies," reminded him of the "meanest sort of gipsies" often seen in England. But he was much struck by the Choctaw chief who had "sent in his card to me," and proved to be an impressive figure in an ordinary suit who was well-read and especially fond of Scott's "The Lady of the Lake." "On my telling him that I regretted not to see him in his own attire," Dickens writes, "he threw up his right arm, for a moment, as though he were brandishing some heavy weapon, and answered, as he let it fall again, that his race were losing many things besides their dress, and would soon be seen upon the earth no more: but he wore it at home, he added proudly."

Dickens was also moved, in Pennsylvania, by a display of "treaties made from time to time with the poor Indians, signed by the different chiefs at the period of their ratification, and preserved in the office of the Secretary to the Commonwealth." These signatures, "traced of course by their own hands, are rough drawings of the creatures or weapons they were called after. Thus, the Great Turtle makes a crooked pen-and-ink outline of a great turtle; the Buffalo sketches a buffalo; the War Hatchett sets a rough image of that weapon for his mark. So with the Arrow, the Fish, the Scalp, The Big Canoe, and all of them." Dickens continues:

> I could not but think—as I looked at these feeble and tremulous productions of hands which could draw the longest arrow to the head in a stout elk-horn bow, or split a bead or feather with a rifle-ball—of Crabbe's musings over the Parish Register, and the irregular scratches made with a pen by men who would plough a lengthy furrow straight from end to end. Nor could I help bestowing many sorrowful thoughts upon the simple warriors whose hands and hearts were set there, in all truth and honesty; and who only learned in course of time from white men how to break their faith, and quibble out of forms and bonds. I wonder, too, how many times the credulous Big Turtle, or trusting Little Hatchett, had put his mark to treaties which were falsely read to him, and had signed away, he knew not what, until it went and cast him loose upon the new possessors of the land, a savage indeed.

Dickens was hard on his hosts in the *American Notes*. But he had always been "a natural American," as Michael Slater observed in 1978, and therefore "always had just the same love/hate relationship with America as he had with the country of his birth." Writes Slater:

In his touchy pride, his ruthless energy, his unwavering belief in the rewards of industry, his rejection of the past, and his faith in the future, Dickens was very much an American. Had he not been so American in his idealism in 1842, moreover, he would have never been so bitterly bewildered and disappointed by the imperfections he found obtruding themselves on him as he travelled around the country. With a much deeper truth than the late President Kennedy claiming to be a Berliner, Dickens might have said,

'I am an American.'

PREPARATORY SCHOOL FOR FAST MEN (2).
SMOKING CLASS——BY PUFFENOUGH PUFFIN.

CAPSULE

MARTIN CHUZZLEWIT.

1843-44

"There are some men," observes the narrator of *Nicholas Nickleby*, "who, living with the one object of enriching themselves, no matter by what means, and being perfectly conscious of the baseness and rascality of the means which they will use every day towards this end, affect nevertheless—even to themselves—a high tone of moral rectitude, and shake their heads and sigh over the depravity of the world."

The narrator continues: "some of the craftiest scoundrels that ever walked the earth, or rather—for walking implies, at least, an erect posture and the bearing of a man—that ever crawled and crept through life by its dirtiest and narrowest ways, will gravely jot down in diaries the events of every day, and keep a regular debtor and creditor account with Heaven, which shall always show a floating balance in their own favor."

This passage in *Nickleby* directly forecasts the appearance of Seth Pecksniff, the bombastic scoundrel who figures prominently in *Martin Chuzzlewit*, the novel that Dickens himself considered a singular achievement, and that some of his contemporaries, including Wilkie Collins, ranked among his best. Pecksniff personifies what early Victorians would have called "cant"—bald self-interest badly disguised as righteous concern.

Pecksniff is full of aggressive impulses he conceals behind a façade of strained geniality and a flow of maxims that tend, not incidentally, to confirm his own self-proclaimed virtues. "I may be a hypocrite," he admits, "but I am not a brute." Like Dickens' other theatrical, self-deceiving figures— Vincent Crummles, William Dorrit, and Wilkins Micawber—Pecksniff "was in the frequent habit of using any word that occurred to him of having a good sound." "Money," Pecksniff asserts, "is the root of all evil"—never mind that he is obsessed with money, and plots to get his own piece of Old Martin Chuzzlewit's large estate.

Old Martin, despite his wealth, really does hate money. He finds it an encumbrance and a curse. Money, he complains, has poisoned his familial and personal relations. "Treachery, deceit, and low design; hatred of competitors, real or fancied, for my favor; meanness, falsehood, baseness, and servility"—"these," he asserts, "are the beauties which my wealth has brought to light."

It's a recurrent theme in Dickens' fiction: no major English writer was drawn so frequently to the subject of money or brooded so famously on its warping effects on society and individual lives. Dickens also knew the allure of money and, after a childhood wrecked by his family's lack of it, made absolutely certain he would always have enough of the stuff around.

From the very start of his career, he'd been acutely attuned to the business of writing, negotiating hard with publishers over percentages and rights. He died a rich man.

Dickens was also surprised, however, to find that his fame, and his renown for charitable works, had made him a large target for spongers of all kinds. In addition to support-ing his parents and his cash-strapped younger brothers, Dickens was over-whelmed with letters from strangers pleading for, even demanding, funds. In 1846 Dickens asked his *Daily News* associate W.H. Wills to respond to a "Mrs. What's-her-name" whose "audacity" in this regard was "re-markable, even to me, who am posi-tively bullied, and all but beaten, by these people." Please tell her, asked Dickens, that "if I were the wealthi-est nobleman in England I could not keep pace with one-twentieth part of the demands upon me."

In his 1850 essay, "The Begging-Letter Writer," Dickens offers a composite picture of these special pleaders and their often shameless requests. He presents a figure that "has besieged my door at all hours of the day and night," and has "fought my servant," and has "followed me out of town into the country." This beggar has "wanted a great coat to go to India in; a pound to set him up in life for ever; a pair of boots to take him to the coast of China; a hat to get him into a permanent situation under government. He has frequently been exactly seven-and-sixpence short of independence."

The begging-letter writer, in his variety of guises, has accumulated dozens of excuses and curious needs. He "has had two children who have never grown up," a brother who "went into business with him, and ran away with the money," a landlord who "has never shown a spark of human feel-ing." He has joined the military, and for some reason "wants a cheese." He is "informed by the sergeant that it is essential to his prospects in the regi-ment that he should take out a single Gloucester cheese, weighing from twelve to fifteen pounds. Eight or nine shillings would buy it. He does not ask for money ... but if he calls at nine tomorrow morning may he hope to find a cheese?"

Martin Chuzzlewit also revisits Dickens' letdown during his recent American tour: he shoots back at the newspaper and pamphlet-writers who used his protests against literary piracy as an excuse to portray him as a greedy and ungrateful young man. Dickens had already exposed the nation's shortcomings in *American Notes,* and here he sends Old Mar-tin's nephew, Young Martin, on an-other American excursion where, ac-cording to Dickens, newspapers are called the *New York Stabber,* the *New York Sewer,* and the *New York Peeper:* they specialize in slander.

Americans, as Young Martin sees them, specialize in boasting, self-promotion, and self-deceit. It's a na-tion full of Pecksniffs, apparently. Martin is forever being introduced to "one of the most remarkable men in the country," but what he finds is a

1843-44

great many bores. ("I am quite serious when I say that I do believe there are not on the whole earth," Dickens told John Forster in a letter during his first American tour, "so many intensified bores as in these United States. No man can form an adequate idea of the real meaning of the word, without coming here.") Americans, Martin gathers, are better at drinking than talking, more inclined to speechify than to converse. They are not especially gifted in the social graces or the conversational arts. They are obsessed with money instead.

Martin's American visit allows Dickens to underline the larger aim, in *Chuzzlewit*, of satirizing selfishness—while showing the way selfishness breeds greed. In America, Dickens found taking shape all that he feared about a future in which "Mammonism," to use Carlyle's term, would grow pervasive, and the commodification of everything would eventually take hold. "Dollars," muses Martin among the Yankees. "All their cares, joys, hopes, affections, virtues, and associations seemed to be melted down into dollars." Men "were weighed by their dollars, gauged by their dollars; life was auctioneered, appraised, put up, and knocked down for its dollars."

Slaves, of course, were explicitly measured by their dollar value. In *American Notes*, the younger Dickens does not hide his contempt for slavery, and he points to its corrosive effect on the culture at large. "'Cash for Negroes,'" he notices with disgust, "'Cash for Negroes, Cash for Negroes,' is the heading of advertisements in great capitals down the long columns of the crowded journals.") In *Chuzzlewit*, Dickens offers up the Norris family as the focus of this attack. Snobbish and rich, the Norrises are "the bright particular stars of an exalted New York sphere." They are racists as well. "Mr. Norris the son," at the mere thought of interracial contact, "made a wry face and dusted his fingers as Hamlet might after getting rid of Yorick's skull, just as though he had at that moment touched a Negro and some of the black had come off upon his hands."

A few paragraphs later, Dickens underlines the family's hypocrisy when, with characteristic blunt irony, he brings on General Fladdock, a family friend, who has just come back from "that a-mazing Eu-rope" where he regretted "an absence of a moral dignity" found in the "artificial barriers set up between man and, the division of the human race into court cards and plain cards of every denomination—into clubs, diamonds, spades, anything but hearts!" But Fladdock and the Norrises are appalled to learn that Martin, crossing over from that "a-mazing Eu-rope," had been required to "observe strict economy." "I took my passage," Martin admits, "in the steerage."

The general is shocked. "He, Fladdock, Fladdock in full militia uniform, Fladdock the General, Fladdock, the caressed of foreign noblemen, expected to know a fellow who had come over in the steerage of line-of-packet ship, at the cost of four pound ten! And meeting that fellow in the very sanctuary of New York fashion, and nestling in the bosom of the New York aristocracy! He almost laid his hand upon his sword."

Dickens, though, always saw that the human propensity for self-congratulation is not limited to bores from "exalted spheres." It's nearly universal, this comforting sense of feeling superior to somebody else. Sairey Gamp, the sodden midwife and night nurse who, with Pecksniff, lights up *Martin Chuzzlewit*, talks spiritedly of her dubious accomplishments; she even invents a character, Mrs. Harris, whose prime role is to extol the odd virtues of Sairey Gamp.

Mrs. Gamp famously represents Dickens comedy, and that comedy, as V.S. Pritchett once observed, grows out of the fact that London itself is, in many ways, "the chief character" of much of his fiction. "Its fogs," he writes, "its smoke, its noise, its courts, officers, bricks, slums, and docks, its gentilities and its crimes, have a quasi-human body. London is seen as the sum of the fantasies and dreams of its inhabitants."

"It is," Pritchett continues, "a city of speeches and voices. The comedy will be in the fusion of the city's dream life and its realities. So will the committal to moral indignation. What we precisely find in this comedy is the people's projection of their self-esteem, the attempt to disentangle the self from the ineluctable London situation; they take on the dramatic role of solitary pronouncers. All Dickens' characters, comic or not, issue personal pronouncements that magnify their inner life. Some are crude like Podsnap, others are subtle like Pecksniff or poetic like Micawber, unbelievable like Skimpole, aristocratic casuists like the father of the Marshalsea, glossy like the Veneerings. All are actors; quip or rhetoric is second nature to them. They are strange, even mad, because they speak as if they were the only persons in the world."

Dickens would always set virtue against vice; invariably, his novels offer good and generous figures to set against the vultures, self-promoters, and cads. *Martin Chuzzlewit* particularly favors Tom Pinch, "an ungainly, awkward-looking man, extremely short-sighted, and prematurely bald," who "might have been almost any age between sixteen and sixty." Pinch, like Little Nell, carries his resolute innocence into a rough and indifferent world. Pecksniff, not surprisingly, bullies and abuses Tom Pinch. But Dickens spares him. And just as Pecksniff is punished (turned into a "drunken, squalid, begging-letter-writing man," no less) Tom finds himself surrounded by tranquility and love. His calm decency merits its own apt reward.

Christmas Stories

....

As she grew older, Dickens' eldest daughter, Kate, also grew tired of finding her father linked so frequently with the merry spirit of the Christmas season. When she learned that her friend George Bernard Shaw was writing a book about Dickens, Katey asked him please to "make the public understand that my father was not a joyous, jocose gentleman walking about the world with a plum pudding and a bowl of punch."

And yet, since then, Dickens' connection to Christmas has only grown stronger, particularly in recent years. In December

2006, a theatre critic in the American Midwest, struck by an array of Dickens-related events, suggested that the author of *A Christmas Carol* would "undoubtedly be astonished to know that 136 years after his death, he has become a symbol of secular Christmas second only to Santa Claus."

Dickens is often described as "the man who invented Christmas." But it's not quite true. In his 2005 book *Christmas and Charles Dickens*, David Parker demonstrates that, even before the Victorian era, Christmas was widely considered "a key festival in the lives of most English people." Its songs and stories, its traditional foods and gifts, its religious and social rites may have been considered vulgar among the patrician classes. But "festive revelry" was very much a part of lower-and middle-class life. Dickens, certainly, had celebrated Christmas with his family, and it's likely he associated the holiday with the sense of stability and hope that (along with his sense of childhood itself) had vanished suddenly. In any event, Dickens did not "revive a defunct or flagging festival," as Parker writes. He "made a popular festival mean more."

A Christmas Carol is very probably Dickens' most representative work—a microcosm of the great Dicksensian world. It attacks selfishness and political apathy. It offers the hope of moral change and redemption. Of course it's sentimental—but it's satirical too. And it's full of strange and absurd touches—splendid bits of personification and grotesquerie that, once read, never quite leave the mind. You might remember "the great, round, pot-bellied baskets of

chestnuts" that Scrooge spots during his nocturnal tour with the Ghost of Christmas Present. They're accompanied by "ruddy, brown-faced, broad-girthed Spanish Onions, shining in the fatness of their growth like Spanish Friars, and winking from their shelves in wanton slyness at the girls as they went by, and glanced demurely at the hung-up mistletoe."

As Scrooge discovers, the revelers of Christmas, those happy souls out joking about and throwing snowballs, will also happily consume "piles of filberts, mossy and brown, recalling, in their fragrance, ancient walks among the woods, and pleasant shuffling ankle deep through withered leaves," and "Norfolk Biffins, squab and swarthy, setting off the yellow of the oranges and lemons, and, in the great compactness of their juicy persons, urgently entreating and beseeching to be carried home in paper bags and eaten after dinner."

Initially, Dickens had published *A Christmas Carol* in a smart, neatly-bound illustrated edition that succeeded brilliantly as a keepsake, but—because of its high production costs—failed to turn much of a profit, for Dickens at least. The publishers of *Parley's Illuminated Library* promptly issued a popular pirated edi-

tion, much to Dickens' ire. He sued the publishers, who duly declared bankruptcy, leaving Dickens with more anger directed at lawyers and the courts. "I shall never forget the expense, and anxiety, and horrible injustice of the *Carol* case, wherein, in asserting the plainest right on earth, I was really treated as if I were the robber instead of the robbed."

In 1844, Dickens published a second Christmas book, *The Chimes*. Its central character is a small, decent, hard-working man whose life, an endless grind, is much enlivened by small dramas and delights, like having an extra shilling in his pocket or hearing the church bells chime. Trotty, getting old, still fancies himself "as strong as a lion" and he's generally good-natured, except when he ponders the plight of the poor. "I don't know what we poor are coming to," he tells his daughter Meg, the love of his life. "Lord send we may be coming to something better in the New Year nigh upon us!"

"I can't make out whether we have any business on the face of the earth, or not. Sometimes I think we must have—a little; and sometimes I think we must be intruding. I get so puzzled sometimes that I am not even able to make up my mind whether there is any good at all in us, or whether we are born bad. We seem to be dreadful things; we seem to give a deal of trouble; we are always being complained of and guarded against. One way or other, we fill the papers."

Trotty is made content in the end, surrounded by love and good cheer. (This is a Christmas story, after all.) First, however, Dickens makes him encounter some frightening things, including a pair of pompous windbags, representatives of the ruling class, and a team of goblins who live in the church tower and temporarily turn Trotty into a phantom of sorts who must witness the terrible hardships that tend to befall poor people, including his beloved Meg.

George Cruikshank's picture of Christmas feasting

Alderman Cute, the first windbag, relishes his official role and his power over the powerless. He's tired of all "the nonsense talked about Want," and all the talk about so many people being "hard up." The poor must be "put down," he declares, along with everything else that irritates Alderman Cute. Sir Joseph Bowley, meanwhile, presents himself as the "poor man's friend." And he promises, in return for their subservience, his measured benevolent regard. The poor, then, have no voice and few choices in a world run by the likes of Bowley and Cute. Bowley's message to Trotty is thus: "Go forth erect into the cheerful morning air, and—stop there. Live hard and temperately, be respectful, exercise your self-denial, bring up your family on next to nothing, pay your rent as regularly as the clock strikes, be punctual in your dealings … and you may trust to me to be your Friend and Father."

Like *A Christmas Carol*, *The Chimes* seeks to humanize and dignify the struggling urban poor: It explicitly attacks the smug indifference of the monied class. Dickens' next Christmas story, *The Cricket on the Hearth* (1845), is not explicitly political, but it also seeks to show how habits of selfishness and sourness can make a man monstrous to others and to himself. The morally obtuse figure here is "Tackleton, the toy-merchant, pretty generally known as Gruff and Tackleton—for that was the firm, though Gruff had been bought out long ago; only leaving his name, and some said his nature, according to its dictionary meaning." Tackleton, notes the narrator, probably should have been a "money lender or a sharp attorney, or a Sheriff's officer, or a broker; he might have sown his discontented oats in his youth, and, after having had the full run of himself in ill-natured transactions, might have turned out amiable, at last, for the sake of a little freshness and novelty."

Instead, he was a toymaker who didn't care much for children and who hated toys. In his "malice," he manufactured "appalling masks; hideous, hairy, red-eyed Jacks in Boxes; Vampire kites; demoniacal tumblers who wouldn't lie down, and were perpetually flying forward, to stare infants out of countenance." And this is how Tackleton looks: a man with "his hands tucked into the bottom of his pants, and his whole sarcastic ill-conditioned self peering out of one little corner of one little eye, like the concentrated essence of any number of ravens."

Tackleton visits a kindly married couple, the Peerybingles, who have allowed a cricket to find a little space in their house and to chirp away cheerfully. For the Peerybingles, this noisy insect is a symbol of good luck and a blessing to their house. Tackleton, of course, finds it annoying. And all this talk of domestic tranquility is bosh. "Bah! What's a home?" he says to John Peerybingle. "Four walls a ceiling! Why don't you kill that Cricket? I would! I always do. I hate their noise."

"You kill your crickets, eh?" says John.

"Scruch 'em, sir," returned the other, setting his heel heavily on the floor.

True to the spirit of the Christmas books, Tackleton is redeemed, made aware that he was for years "a miserable idiot,"

and eager at last to indulge his own capacity for being jovial. When last we see him, he is feasting and dancing in a happy party with the Peerybingles in their cozy home while the cricket chirps merrily along.

The Battle of Life (1846) is also a tale of conversion. The learned Doctor Jeddler isn't as wretchedly mean as Tackleton or Scrooge; but he, too, is sadly unable to enjoy the delights and happy surprises of life. He makes his home on a battlefield where once "the stream ran red" with human blood. Jeddler, a widower, is "a great philosopher, and the heart and mystery of his philosophy was, to look upon the world as a gigantic practical joke; as something too absurd to be considered seriously, by any rational man." Human beings, he thinks, are hopelessly foolish; and in his private zone of contemplation, he keeps himself above the ridiculous fray.

But Jeddler, too, is moved ("It's a world full of hearts," he finally declares) by the devotion his daughters show for each other, and by their shared sense of *joie de vivre*—amply illustrated early in the story. Dickens shows the young women dancing together among the apple-pickers in Jeddler's orchard. The two girls "quite unconstrained and careless, danced in the freedom and gaiety of their hearts." They danced "not like opera-dancers. Not at all. And not like Madame Anybody's finished pupils. Not in the least. It was not quadrille dancing, nor minuet dancing, nor even country-dance dancing. It was neither in the old style, nor the new style, nor the French style, nor the English style: though it may have been, by accident, a trifle in the Spanish style, which is a free and joyous one."

One is struck by how the tone and spirit of these sketches— mixing melodrama, sentiment, and moral satire—survived for so long in the popular art of Britain and the United States. Many of the types Dickens presents here—the cranky miser, the kindly matron, the bookish widower and his vivacious daughters—all lived on in countless Hollywood scripts. There's a long but fairly straight line between Dickens' Christmas books and the films of Frank Capra and Charlie Chaplin. Eleanor Farjeon, in her 1954 introduction to the *Christmas Books*, noted that Chaplin, "better than any genius since Charles Dickens, has known how to use wild laughter congruously with pure pathos."

Social-climbing and Self-delusion

Dickens continued to publish special Christmas stories and tales in his magazines, although these did not necessarily include great servings of mistletoe and pudding. "Going into Society," another "moral fable," as it's been called, differs notably from the earlier

Christmas stories. It isn't sentimental, for one thing, but more darkly comic. Its colloquial narrator, Toby Magsman, is a sideshow operator who tells the story of Mr. Chops, one of his top performers, "a most uncommon small man, with a most uncommon large Ed." Chops has known life's disappointments, not least a broken romance with "the fat lady from Norfolk," who "trifled" with his affections.

Chops, however, yearns to improve himself, to be a figure "in society." After winning the lottery—"twelve thousand odd hundred pound"—he gets his chance and he promptly heads for London in "a chay and four grays with silk jackets." Chops takes lodgings in Pall Mall, where—as Magsman puts it—he "blazed away." But he is disappointed, made aware that "high society" is itself little more than a gaudy show. "Society, taken in the lump," he tells Magsman, "is all dwarfs."

"Going into Society" satirizes pretense, social-climbing, and man's endless capacity for self-delusion. As such, it's closer in spirit to the later novels than to the earlier Christmas tales—or "Masques" as Dickens called them—which "the good-humour of the season justified," and which aimed to "awaken some loving and forebearing thoughts, never out of season in a Christian land."

In fact Dickens, particularly early in his career, directly linked the themes of his fiction with the tenets of his faith. "One of my most constant and most earnest endeavors has been to exhibit in all of my

good people some faint reflections of the teachings of our Great Master." "All of my strongest illustrations," he says elsewhere, "are derived from the New Testament; all of my social abuses are shown as departures from its spirit."

It's not a point that escaped many of Dickens' early admirers. In 1909, one of these readers, a Mr. Edwin Charles, published a protest of the staging of *A Christmas Carol* in a London music hall. "I have no objection to music-halls," Mr. Charles wrote, "but I do not think they are fitted, either by the necessities of their programme or by their environment, for the exploitation of sacred subjects. I regard *A Christmas Carol* as a sacred subject, and I believe there are thousands of other Dickens worshippers who think with me in that respect. It is a sermon, amplifying and exemplifying Holy Writ itself, telling all in a practical and material manner of the newer and higher and holier duties of man to man which Christ came down on earth to teach."

DOMBEY AND SON.

1846-48

In many ways, this is Dickens' most Victorian novel—the one contemporary readers are most likely not to finish, or even start. When it was published, however, *Dombey and Son*—in which a young boy dies and his hardhearted father, a businessman, softens and mends—was a decisive success. Dickens' literary rival, William Thackeray, was apparently quite moved by the novel's depiction of young Paul's death. He called it "stupendous" and "unsurpassed." "There's no writing against such power as this," Thackeray asserted. "One has no chance!"

Dombey marks a transition for Dickens. He starts moving away from romping picaresque romances to more recognizably real central characters and more convincing plots. Paul Dombey, the title character, runs a shipping firm. He is "rather bald, rather red," one of those "close-shaved close-cut monied gentlemen who are glossy and crisp like new bank notes."

Money pervades *Dombey*. The novel indicts what Thomas Carlyle called "Mammon-worship," a persistent and "melancholy" creed he found much in evidence in the Britain of his day. Mammonism brings the notion that "cash-payment" is "the sole relation of human beings." This, however, "has as yet made nobody rich." Among both the poor and the wealthy, Carlyle wrote, "instead of noble thrift and plenty, there is idle luxury alternating with mean scarcity and inability. We have sumptuous garnitures for our Life, but have forgotten to live in the middle of them. It is an enchanted wealth; no man of us can yet touch it. The class of men who feel they are truly better off by means of it, let them give us their name!"

Dickens' title character knows many things about money and almost nothing about life. He is a widower with two children, Florence and Paul. The girl doesn't interest him much: after all, "in the capital of the House's name and dignity," she is merely "a piece of base coin that couldn't be invested." Young Paul, however, is valuable as Dombey's heir. Dombey carefully prepares the boy, enrolling him in what he assumes is quite a good school—Doctor Blimber's Academy in Brighton.

Blimber is not limber, but bloated and blustering. He's a pedagogue, with no understanding of children and little sense of how best to run a school. His academy is like "a great hot-house, in which there was a forcing apparatus always at work." His students are force-fed facts, not unlike Squeers' boy inmates at Dotheboys Hall. Dickens describes Blimber in machine-like terms: "His walk was stately, and calculated to impress the

1846-48

juvenile mind with solemn feelings. It was a sort of march; but when the Doctor put out his right foot, he gravely turned upon his axis, with a semicircular sweep towards the left; and when he put out his left foot, he turned in the same manner to the right. So that he seemed, at every stride he took, to look about him as though he were saying, 'Can anybody have the goodness to indicate any subject, in any direction, on which I am uninformed? I rather think not.'"

The method doesn't suit young Paul. He's a frail and sensitive child, affectionate and dreamy. Biographers have long compared him to Dickens' son Sydney, who had charmed and amused his parents with his curiously contemplative, un-childlike air. But Paul also recalls Dickens himself, the sickly boy who passed long hours in the company of books. Paul is, effectively, an orphan—just as the younger Dickens saw himself. Over the years, however, he has struck many readers as the male Little Nell, Dickens' somewhat overdrawn depiction of a child too pure and too good-hearted for such a ruthless world.

Dombey remarries. His second wife, Edith, does not melt the stone-like Dombey heart. She is not demure, but "willful," and Dickens sympathizes with her plight. He understands the resentments that have built up in Edith over many years. Like Estella in *Great Expectations*—like many children in Dickens' fiction—Edith has been badly guided by a flawed and selfish adult. Her mother, Mrs. Skewton, is a domineering hypocrite who long prepared her daughter for the highest bidder. At one point Edith angrily asks her: "What childhood did you ever leave me?" "I was a woman—artful, designing, mercenary, laying snares for men—before I knew myself, or you, or even understood the base and wretched aim of every new display I learnt."

Dombey enjoyed an easy supremacy in his first marriage. "Mr. Dombey, in his cold and lofty arrogance, had borne himself like the removed Being he almost conceived himself to be. He had been 'Mr. Dombey' with her when she first saw him, and was 'Mr. Dombey' when she died. He had asserted his greatness during their whole married life, and she had meekly recognized it. He kept his distant seat on the top of his throne, and she her humble station on its lowest step." Edith, he assumed, would similarly know her place in the family hierarchy.

Dickens does hint that, deep down in Dombey, a small, warming flame burns. He turns up for his wedding in a rather dandified state, sporting "fawn-colored pantaloons" and a lilac waistcoat. Even his hair was, according to whispers, curled. Once wed, however, Dombey returns to form in the only role he's known. But Edith is unhappy in her part, and their marriage becomes a war. *Dombey and Son* starts to remind one of John Galsworthy's *The Forsythe Saga*, which began to appear in 1906, when readers were generally more accustomed to the frank depiction of marital problems in novels and plays. In one scene Edith looks "fixedly" at the husband who would keep her enchained. She turns a bracelet "round and round upon her arm; not winding it about with a light, womanly touch, but pressing it over the smooth skin, until the white limb showed a bar of red."

Dickens, famous as a comic writer and a celebrator of cheery domestic life, is here doing something quite different, even a little daring—portraying a respectable but miserable marriage where the threat on infidelity intrudes. Edith's would-be lover is one of Dombey's associates, a stealthy man rendered in cat-like terms. Carker is "feline from sole to crown," His hair and whiskers are like "the coat of a sandy tortoise-shell cat." He has "long nails, nicely pared and sharpened." His teeth are also sharp, and notably large. Dickens calls him "the man of teeth" and in one scene shows him "airing his teeth" as he plots out his plan to make Edith his lover.

Carker ends up badly, but Dombey is redeemed by his daughter Florence's love. His better self blooms. But before the curtain falls, there are fireworks on Dickens' stage. Edith denounces the oily Carker: "What should I say of honour or chastity to you. ...What meaning would it have to you; what meaning would it have from me! But if I tell you that the lightest touch of your hand makes my blood cold with antipathy; that from the hour when I first saw, and hated you, to now, when my instinctive repugnance is enhanced by every minute's knowledge of you I have

since had, you have been a loathsome creature to me which has not its like on earth." As for Carker: "The foam was on his lips; the wet stood on his forehead." If Edith "would have faltered once, for only have a minute, he would have pinioned her." Edith, though, is "as firm as a rock."

Elsewhere the novel's narrator intrudes, as he often does in Dickens' earlier novels, exhorting Dombey to be less rock-like himself. "Awake unkind father! Awake now, sullen man! The time is flitting by; the hour is coming with an angry tread. Awake!"

In 1873, in his review of Forster's biography, the American novelist William Dean Howells expressed a view often found among Dickens' critics. The most popular novelist of his age was "a man of unquestionable genius," but "his material, at its finest, was never of the finest. The melodramatic was his notion of the dramatic, the eloquent was his idea of the poetic; his humor was burlesque; his pathos was never too deep for tears." Howells, who sought to work in a more realistic vein, complained of the "shapelessness" of Dickens' plots, the "unnaturalness of his situations," and the "crudity" of his characters. For Howells, a novel like *Dombey and Son* did little to advance the novel as an art form: it was too "padded," too representative of a fashion in fiction and writing whose time and come and gone.

The Economist, however, had greeted the novel's arrival with enthusiastic praise. Its reviewer was delighted to find that Dickens had

1846-48

given up his editorship of the *Daily News* to turn to literature once more, for "never was there a man so little suited to the wear and tear and vulgar huck-a-buck work of the daily press." And *Dombey*, thought *The Economist*, caught the spirit of the times: "The world of London is filled with cold, stiff, purse-proud men like this, who think, as Dickens says, the earth was made for *Dombey and Son* to trade in, and the sun and moon were made to give them light, and that A.D. has no concern with Anno Domini, but stands for Anno Dombei."

Still, many of Dickens' friends and fellow writers thought the novel had turned too melodramatic and sentimental in its closing chapters. "The last *Dombeys* are infernally bad," complained Harrison Ainsworth in a letter to a friend. William Macready agreed. "I fear dear Dickens," he recorded in his journal, "called to ascertain our feeling about the last number of *Dombey*. I could not speak as I wished, and therefore did not allude to it."

But this novel, upon which Dickens "bestowed all the pains and time at my command upon it," proved both widely popular and highly profitable, and its success convinced Dickens that, artistically, he was on the right path. He was certainly aware of the book's wide appeal. Forster recalls the time that Dickens had rushed back from Paris to visit his son Charley, who had contracted scarlet fever and was the under care of his grandmother, Mrs. Hogarth.

Writes Forster: "An elderly charwoman employed about the place had shown so much sympathy in the family trouble, that Mrs. Hogarth specially told her of the approaching visit, and who it was that was coming to the sick room."

"'Lawk ma'am!' Is the young gentleman upstairs the son of the man that put together *Dombey*?' Reassured upon this point, she explained her question by declaring that she never thought there was a man that could have put together *Dombey*. Being pressed further as to what her notion was of this mystery of a Dombey (for it was known she could not read), it turned out that she lodged at a snuff-shop kept by a person named Douglas, where there were several other lodgers; and that on the first Monday of every month there was a Tea, and the landlord read the month's number of *Dombey*, those only of the lodgers who subscribed to the tea partaking of that luxury, but all having the benefit of the reading; and the impression produced on the old charwoman revealed itself in the remark which she closed her account of it. 'Lawk ma'am! I thought that three or four men must have put together *Dombey*!' Dickens thought there was something of a compliment in this, and was not ungrateful."

The Magnitizer

....

Throughout much of the Victorian era, mesmerism—or animal magnetism, as it was also known—was the subject of much controversy and debate. Its advocates included some well-known physicians, scientist, and writers—including Charles Dickens. They believed, or at least hoped, that mesmerism was not simply a sort of trick, or a fad, but a real scientific breakthrough and a useful therapeutic tool.

Mesmerism paved the way for hypnosis by asserting that the human mind could be effectively mined—and healed—when it entered the state of trance. Moreover skilled mesmerists, some believed, were able to facilitate the flow of healing cosmic forces. Dickens, after some practice, mastered the mesmerist's method just as he had once mastered shorthand. Quite literally, he could put you under his spell.

Mesmerism takes its name from Anton Mesmer, a Viennese physician who, in the 1760s and '70s, attracted a large following in several European cities. Mesmer mixed physics, metaphysics, and highly imaginative speculation. The cosmos, he theorized, was permeated by an invisible magnetic fluid that greatly influenced all plant and animal life. When this "celestial gravity" entered freely into a person, the effect was salubrious—physical and mental health. Blocked forces could, however, produce mental or physical disease.

Magnets, Mesmer theorized, helped stimulate the cosmic flow. To this end, he often utilized a large wooden tub filled with "magnetized water." Once they were immersed, Mesmer directed his patients to grasp one of the iron rods that protruded from the sides of the tub: these, apparently, were like antennas designed to catch and direct the great, invisible, healing waves.

Eventually, however, Mesmer believed himself capable of infusing his subjects directly with his own abundant energy, or "animal magnetism"—thus called because of its supposed connection to the anima, or soul. By all accounts, Mesmer was a compelling figure. He induced his spells with repetitive hand movements and a piercing gaze. He wore special robes patterned with astrological and alchemical symbols. Often, as Mesmer mesmerized, an accompanist quietly played the glass harmonica. Many subjects achieved the trance-like state; some also experienced a series of purportedly purgative convulsions. Inevitably, Mesmer became the subject of suspicion and attack—but not before his adventures in magnetism greatly increased his wealth and renown.

In A Trance

In Britain, interest in mesmerism grew greatly during the 1830s, thanks largely to the efforts of John Elliotson, a leading professor of medicine at London's University College. Elliotson was drawn to the new. Medicine, he argued, must be forever moving forward. He thus championed the use of the stethoscope, and other innovative diagnostic tools. And mesmerism, he insisted, had a huge future in modern medicine. In fact Elliotson, a gifted lecturer and acclaimed mesmerist in his own right, often amazed observers by showing them how, even while undergoing surgery, deeply mesmerized patients felt no pain. Mesmerism, moreover, might well unlock many psychological mysteries, Elliotson explained. Who knew what drives and impulses the skilled mesmerist might reveal? Who knew what dark truths the conscious mind conceals?

Elliotson was very much the sort of man Dickens was inclined to admire and befriend—a confident, rather theatrical, and highly ambitious figure who was not a literary competitor but a star in his own field. Through Elliotson, and another friend, the Reverend Chauncey Townshend (to whom *Great Expectations* is dedicated), Dickens developed his interest in mesmerism; and he too came to believe in its potential as an emerging "science of the mind." Dickens had little or no interest in Mesmer's dotty cosmic theories, spelled out in largely incomprehensible writings, but he was immediately fascinated by the mesmerist's mind-altering, and mind-controlling, powers.

Dickens' earliest subjects included his wife and his sister-in-law Georgina, who—as William Charles Macready's diaries reveal—promptly went into "hysterics" during the procedure. Dickens also tried to magnetize Macready, but the gloomy actor was not game, finding the whole episode "very unpleasant" and certain "it could not effect me."

It did, however, effect Augusta de la Rue, the subject of Dickens' most intensive mesmeric endeavors. Dickens met the de la Rues during his 1844 vast to Italy. Emile de la Rue, a businessman, was a likable, lively conversationalist; Augusta was "an excellent little woman," in Dickens' view. She also suffered, she said, from a host of ailments, and these Charles Dickens, mesmerist, promptly offered to cure.

Extrasensory Perception

From the far distance of today, it would seem that Augusta de la Rue was either severely disturbed; or, that her imagination responded exceedingly well to the attentions of a famous young novelist who obviously found her attractive and alluring. In addition to the "burning and raging" in her head, Augusta told Dickens, she was often rattled by images of a mysterious figure—a "Phantom" who haunted her thoughts and dreams. But mesmerism, she reported, brought real relief, and she was deeply grateful that Dickens was so willing to treat her, even at odd hours of the night.

Dickens, meanwhile, felt so drawn to Augusta that—even from a distance, while both sleeping and awake—he could somehow discern her state of mind. Such extrasensory perception was, some believed, an added function of those mysterious magnetic forces; and Augusta, Dickens now admitted, was "somehow a part of me."

Thus, months later, after he had returned to England and to the routines of work and home, Dickens wrote to Emile to say that he not only missed the easy conviviality of his life in Italy, but also the curious intensity of his mesmeric sessions with Mme de la Rue. "Was I ever an idle man in a plaid coat," Dickens wondered, "basking, day after day, on the box of a traveling carriage with a happy little party? Or is it all a Dream, and did I ever magnetize a little Somebody; with all my heart in her recovery and happiness?"

Although Catherine Dickens submitted regularly to her husband's mesmeric experimentations, she never warmed to his magnetizing other women, particularly a little Somebody called Augusta de la Rue. Anton Mesmer's critics had often charged him with practicing seduction, and many Victorians retained the suspicion that mesmerism was more likely to invite moral depravity than celestial gravity. Dickens resented his wife's suspicion of impropriety, for he long preferred to think of himself as a man more sinned against than sinning, and who was in any event overburdened by his sluggardly spouse. Still, as the years passed and as new passions and causes absorbed him, Dickens found less time for magnetizing his family and friends.

And, inevitably, mesmeromania began to fade. Elliotson's critics grew more vocal in insisting that "animal magnetism" was not, and could never be, scientifically valid. They also alleged that some of Elliotson's best-known subjects were, whether he knew it or not, fakes—amateur actors basking in the rare attention they received while addressing large audiences in a supposed state of trance. Eventually, Elliotson left University Hospital, denouncing his hidebound colleagues and starting a journal, *The Zoist*, devoted to the study and promotion of mesmerism and phrenology, the practice of gauging a person's intelligence and character by measuring and mapping the shape of his skull.

Moreover, mesmerism's promise as an anesthesia vanished as more reliable agents, including chloroform, came to the fore. By the early 20th century the very name mesmerism had acquired a distinctly comic aura, although interest in hypnosis—its less esoteric successor—would, of course, continue to grow.

A Conductor of Words

....

Dickens took the title of his new weekly magazine, begun in 1850, from Shakespeare's *Henry V*: "Familiar in their mouths as *Household Words*." By now, Dickens was himself a household name, making the title apt. It was also much better than Dickens' other suggestions: *Mankind*, *The Household Voice*, and *The Robin*, inspired by Oliver Goldsmith: "The redbreast, celebrated for its affection to mankind, continues with us, the year round."

John Forster and Dickens himself invested financially in *Household Words*, which boasted a strong staff of contributors and editors, including W.H. Wills, who supervised the magazine's daily operations. Wills also collaborated with Dickens on such stories as "Valentine's Day at the Post Office" and "The Metropolitan Protectives," which hailed the "efficiency of the London Police." Wills, though, knew his place: *Household Words* was "Conducted by Charles Dickens," as each issue made prominently clear.

"When I make an objection to any article," Wills once admitted, "I do it suggestively."

Household Words and its successor, *All the Year Round*, were always strictly run along lines Dickens preferred. He used both his fiction and his journalism to expose the neglect and the abuse of the poor and to call for civic institutions better able to meet the needs of a powerful nation changing dramatically by the forces of rapid industrialization. Dickens' publications contend that Britain would be improved and made more humane through education and science—powerful forces to sweep away old "distortions," bar-

barisms, and fears. Although his later novels are often quite dark, Dickens' magazines follow the more optimistic note he struck in the first issue of *Household Words*.

Dickens' "Preliminary Word" assured readers that his publication, appearing in this "summer-dawn of time," would not be merely "utilitarian" in spirit. It would "cherish that light of Fancy which is inherent in the human breast." It would hope to "teach the hardest workers at this whirling wheel of toil, that their lot is not necessarily a moody, brutal fact, excluded from the sympathies and graces of imagination." And it would seek to bring the various classes together and "mutually dispose them to a better understanding." In fact, this hope of respectful cooperation between the classes is at the heart of Dickens' later political views. He was never radical enough for Marxists, anarchists, or others on the far political left. (A disgusted Lenin once famously stormed out of a staging of *The Cricket on the Hearth*.) Dickens, in many ways, fits the profile of a twentieth-century American liberal. But to call him a "compassionate conservative" would also be close to the mark.

George Sala

Household Words, Dickens declared, would not be provincial. It would not "treat of the hopes, the enterprises, triumphs, joys, and sorrows of this country only, but in some degree, of those of every nation upon earth. For nothing can be a source of real interest in one of them, without concerning all the rest." Cynics, he suggests, might scoff at this ambition. But then, negative voices always urge retreat in the face of life's hardest challenges. "All the voices we hear, cry Go on!" For "the road is not so rough that it need daunt our feet: the way is not so steep that we need stop for rest, and, looking faintly down, be stricken motionless. Go on, is all we hear, Go on! In a glow already, with the air from yonder height upon us, and the inspiriting voices joining in this acclamation, we echo back the cry, and go on cheerily!"

In 1850 Dickens also published "the Begging-Letter Writer," an essay that similarly sheds light on his political attitudes. The essay voices disgust with those who persist in looking for handouts

97

and unearned favors; who, instead of exercising their own earnest efforts, nurse their greed and sharpen their manipulative skills. Such people, Dickens stresses, deserve nothing but scorn. The truly poor, however, do need the attention of writers, editors and other influential figures—provided these leaders of thought turn less readily to censure than to concerted efforts at improving the commonweal. "Life must be held sacred among us in more ways than one, Dickens writes, "sacred, not merely from the murderous weapon, or the subtle poison, or the cruel blow, but sacred from preventable diseases, distortions, and pains." "Physical life" must be respected, Dickens writes, "moral life comes next. What will not content a Begging-Letter writer for a week, would educate a score of children for a year. Let us give all we can; let us give more than ever. Let us do all we can; let us do more than ever."

Percy Fitzgerald

Dickens wanted no interference with his magazine's operation—and no distractions from the written word. *Household Words* was not illustrated. In a crowded field of daily newspapers and monthly journals, *Household Words* and *All the Year Round* took the high road. Dickens was not, as J.B. Priestly put, "cynically cajoling money out of a lot of half-wits." Probably most of his readers were, he knew, educated members of the aspiring middle-class. They were civil servants, clerics, schoolteachers, office managers, and the like—the sort of people who bought books and sometimes attended concerts and plays; who travelled a bit, or at least wanted to; who thought about politics and kept an interest in public affairs. In many ways, *Household Words* was the Victorian *New Yorker*—an intelligent but accessible mix of fiction, feature writing, commentary and quality prose.

Happy Boldness

Dickens sought out many well-known writers and journalists, including George Sala, whose "The Key of the Street" (1851) was widely noticed and represents the sort of article Dickens looked for. Sala offers a first-person account of spending the night in the guise a poor Londoner who, with no place to live, must sleep rough wherever he can—in a doorway or a bush, huddled in his coat or on a pile of rags. Sala describes passing, as if invisible, through a crowd leaving the opera. Sporting white kid gloves, their lorgnettes still in their hands, they cheerfully hail the cabs that will whisk them to warm feather beds in comfortable homes. Sala, however, ends up on "a bench under a tree," where he also finds a young man, "half-naked" and without shoes, sleeping soundly but roused awake when the "Horse-Guards clock strikes five." "He wakes, eyes me for a moment, and muttering 'hard lines, mate,' turns to sleep again. In the mysterious free-masonry of misery, he calls me 'mate.'"

Like Percy Fitzgerald, Sala was a prolific but uneven writer who benefitted considerably from his association with *Household Words*. In ways large and small, Sala admitted, Dickens improved the work of his contributors. Sala once wrote about living in Erith, Kent, which he called "Sherith," a "blunderingly transparent disguise." But Dickens couldn't resist a Dickensian touch and, "with happy boldness" as Sala recounts, "changed the name to Dumbledowndeary."

Still, like other contributors, Sala was somewhat annoyed that nearly all of the pieces in *Household Words* appeared anonymously, and that—as a result—many readers assumed the best pieces were Dickens' own. In the 1850s Sala bought, in a Paris bookstall, *Les Nouveaux Contes de Charles Dickens*. It included "The Key of the Street." In newspaper circles, Sala wrote, it was "pretty well known" he wrote for *Household Words*, but "beyond that I might have been a writer of auction-summaries, or a compiler of births, deaths, and marriages, for aught that the great reading public knew or cared."

The reading public, Dickens believed, required a clearer picture of public institutions claiming to do good; many articles in *Household Words* concerned schools, prisons, and asylums for the mentally ill. Education, in fact, is one of Dickens' most persistent concerns as both a novelist and a journalist: both *Household Words* and *All the Year Round* turn frequently to the subject of schools. In an early essay in *Household Words*, "A Sample of the Old School by an Old Boy," Percival Leigh expresses Dickens' own belief when he notes that "I knew then, as well as I know now, how worse than foolish and idiotic was the notion of whipping a boy into parrot-learning." "We best remember the ideas which we delight to dwell upon." Thus, "the proper way of imparting knowledge is to make it as pleasant as possible, or if this cannot be done, to administer it by degrees."

For both of Dickens' magazines, the pedagogic emphasis on science and "facts" cannot be sufficient in itself, especially in the early grades; educators should not lose sight of the role of the imagination—or "Fancy"—in the wholesome development of human beings. "Rational Schools" (1852) written by Wills and the prolific Henry Morley for *Household Words*, recounts their visit to one of the "Birkbeck Schools" founded by William Ellis on the Utilitarian principles of John Stuart Mill. The article commends these schools for tending to the needs of intellectually curious children, many from poor or modest homes. Still, the method's heavy emphasis on logic, ratiocination, and the digestion of "facts" added up to a warped approach. The "imaginative faculty" insists the article (two years before the publication of *Hard Times*) must, like "religious principles," be cultivated carefully in children, for this is "no less important to their own happiness and that of society than their knowledge of things and reasons; and it should be steadily borne in mind that no amount of political economy, and no working of figures, will or ever can do without them."

Household Words ran many pieces on the institutional care of the mentally ill, in both England and abroad. There's a certain voyeuristic element to these articles, and touches of black humor: Dickens, as John Carey amply illustrates in *The Violent Effigy* (1972), had a persistent interest in all forms of human abnormality and in gruesome death. (Dickens, after all, was a man who, when visiting Paris, made regular visits to the city morgue, where unidentified bodies were openly displayed.)

Still, these articles are sobering, prompting the suspicion that, in 19th-century Britain, abuse and cruel neglect of the mentally disabled was more common than not. One article, "The Treatment of the Insane," presumably based on the observations of a physician, draws on letters and other documents not originally intended for public scrutiny; in one, the steward of a County Lunatic Asylum shows himself so miserly and budget-conscious that he hopes to expend as little as possible for clothing for "a pauper lunatic"—a fifteen-year-old boy who had hitherto been confined, behind bars, in "what we call a strait waistcoat." Another letter, sent to the asylum administrator, is from the barely literate relative of "a poor woman who had previously suffered from severe attacks of mania." This writer asserts that her "sistar" is "in a very bad stat of life," having been farmed out by her parish to unsupervised handlers who keep her cuffed and chained on a sack of straw. "These men," she is certain, "are very unjest in their werks."

For *Household Words*, such practices showed that "idiots" (as they were generally called) were still forced to live in the dark ages, and that—in the name of progress—more enlightened and compassionate forms of mental health care must be pursued. "It is not enough to repeat the celebrated epitaph on an idiot," urges *Household Words*, "and to hope that his privations here will be made up to him hereafter. We must lessen these privations to the utmost by the careful application of science in understanding his case; and of skill, and inexhaustible patience and love in treating it."

Expanded Bells

For both *Household Words* and *All the Year Round*, science was a blessing, pointing the way to a more enlightened and humane world in the years to come. *Household Words* praises the efforts of the Greenwich Observatory and the Hunterian Museum, where nature's wonders could be seen and the benign goals of science pursued. Other articles—"What Is Sand?" "The Chemistry of a Pint of Beer"—cast light on the complex composition of commonplace things. The microscope is celebrated in an energetic, unsigned article in *All the Year Round*, for this device reveals a startling new slant on the world, and the fact that (for example) "the human hair is a singularly beautiful thing to look at..." It is "made of successive layers, or overlapping cells, gradually tapering to a point like the thinnest and most infinitely twisted paper cone." But "the prettiest hair of all is the bat's." It is like

an immense number of trumpet-shaped flowers set one within the other— a living chain of expanded bells, most beautiful to behold. The hair of the Indian bat is even more flower-like and elegant than that of its English cousin, as the lips of the 'flowers' are closer together, more pointed, and more feathery in the growth. It is to the English bat's what a double flower is to a single, or a garden flower to a wild one.

Hive bees, the microscope shows:

> Have slender pointed hairs upon the head, each hair beset with a number of subordinate short hairs set on in spirals: on the leg, the yellow hairs which we can see with the naked eye turn out to be strong curved horny spines,scored obliquely like a butcher's steel, and used as combs for gathering, storing, and scraping out the pollen. Besides his combs, the bee carries two baskets in his thighs, which baskets are the perfection of such implements, being smooth inside, of undeniable form, and staked up with strong spines: in short, the very ideal of such baskets we should use for carrying pollen or flower grain.

Of course, "all sorts of theories have held ground successively, respecting the feet of flies":

> First they were suckers, and they walked by means of exhaustion and atmospheric pressure; then they were grappling irons, and they hooked themselves on to microscopic inequalities by means of invisible hooks; then they were glue pots and exuded a natural gum, which gummed the insect at every step; now we believe they are assumed to be all three: claws, or spines, to hook; pads, or cushions, to preserve them from abrasion (these pads were the original suckers); hairlets as sucking disks, that exude a certain moisture,—all these hypotheses are found to be true, as always happens in cases when truth unrolls itself in sections.

The "naturalists" are also unrolling truth, as *All the Year Round* points out, disclosing man's ancestral link to other primates. "An Ugly Likeness" (1861) notes that the gorilla cannot be surpassed for "unsightliness, fierceness, strength, and hatred." But its skeleton "makes a far nearer approach to the human skeleton than that of any known animal living or extinct." Clearly, "this near approximation is not flattering," unless we regard it "as showing how completely our animal structure is consistent with the most hateful animal development that can be conceived, and how entirely we are redeemed from being devils by that breathing into our nostrils the breath of intellectual existence and capacity by which man becomes a living soul."

Dickens' magazines are patriotic, and while they repeatedly attack governmental incompetence, they do not question the goals of the British Empire, which is seen as a force of progress throughout the world. Still, they are not chauvinistic, or unwilling to credit the diverse discoveries and accomplishments of other countries. The Belgians, thus, are hailed (in another article by Henry Morley) for the superiority of their railways: "I take the liberty to observe (not altogether without a pang of wounded patriotism) that a third class carriage on a Belgian railway is infinitely superior in comfort and accommodation to a second class carriage on a British railway. It has more air, more light, more conveniences. It has seats so contrived that no man's knees are necessarily in the lap of his fat friend opposite."

The French, not surprisingly, are hailed for their fashion sense—another area in which the English have much to learn. Look from "your window in Paris," advises an 1859 article in *All the Year Round*, and "observe the first fifty women who pass." They may not all be beautiful; "but then, what a toilette!"

> Not only suitable for the season, but to the age and complexion of the wearer. How neat the feet and hands! How well the clothes are put on, and, more than all, how well they suit each other. Not one colour swearing at another colour. We have been imitating the French for centuries in the matter of dress; yet, how little we have in learning from them? If we were asked what would secure success in dress, we should answer, Freshness, before all things; better a clean muslin than tumbled satin. A lady once held up a collar and said, 'Is it soiled?' 'Yes.' 'Why you never looked at it.' 'No; but if there is any doubt, it *is* soiled.'

> Both *Household Words* and *All the Year Round* often criticized the corruption of politics, the mediocrity of the theater, the fraudulence of advertising, and the persistent fondness for war among Europe's ruling elite. Still, both publications did emphasize the necessity for hopefulness and sincere endeavor in this "summer-dawn of time."

An 1850 article on William Wordsworth is especially revealing. Wordsworth, who had recently died, was praised for his poetry and his significant presence in an earlier era of "social and civil revolutions." But Wordsworth, the great poet of the Lake Country, had grown imperious and aloof in more recent years; the essay's author, William Weir, notes that Wordsworth had opposed the growth of railroads and had ungallantly "battled tourists" who had "come to share with him the healthful pleasures of the mountain and the lake," which he would have reserved for "the patent right for the few."

Wordsworth, regrettably, "did not understand, and therefore could not appreciate the ennobling tendencies of the social and scientific career on which this age has entered—an age into which he lingered, rather than to which he belonged."

DAVID COPPERFIELD.

1849-50

David Copperfield was Charles Dickens' favorite Dickens novel. Told in the first person, it is much more than thinly veiled autobiography. Still, *David Copperfield* reconstructs many elements from the author's life. Its title character finds himself without parents at a young age. He briefly attends a middling school. He studies shorthand, works as a political reporter, and blithely enters into an impossible marriage. He becomes a writer and sets forth on a successful career. *David Copperfield,* moreover, offers up many of Dickens' best-known characters, including Wilkins Micawber, Uriah Heep, and the Murdstones—Edward and his "metallic" sister Jane—who mask their will-to-power behind a pronounced concern for domestic order and religious propriety.

The Murdstones are the most infamous targets in Dickens' long attack on organized creeds that stress sin and obedience over mercy, forgiveness, and love. "The gloomy taint that was in the Murdstone blood, darkened the Murdstone religion, which was austere and wrathful," and grew from the notion—always absurd to a liberal Protestant like Dickens—that children are inherently evil, "a swarm of little vipers." Edward Murdstone is David's stepfather, a mechanical man with a "shallow black eye." "I want a better word to an express an eye," David explains, "that has no depth in it to be looked into— which, when it is abstracted seems, from some peculiarity of light, to be disfigured, for a moment at a time, by a cast."

The Murdstones present themselves as pillars of virtue, but they like to pick on people much weaker than themselves. David is still quite young when Murdstone bullies and beats him, and David's widowed mother, Clara, is sensitive and insecure. After marrying Murdstone for security and a home for her son, she finds herself a prisoner instead. "My mother was the victim always," David observes. She apologizes constantly to her oppressors, begging "pray let us be friends. I couldn't live under coldness or unkindness." But the Murdstones favor coldness. Being cold is the only pleasure they know. David always feels their acrimony. When the Murdstones watch him, it is "like the fascination of two snakes on a wretched young bird."

David Copperfield is very interested in the way people invent themselves—or permit themselves to be invented by others. Like other Dickens novels, it tends to place characters in two categories—weak and strong. Weak characters, the novel suggests, often find ways of masking their weakness. But theatricality, the novel shows, pervades human life. The novel's best-known character, Wilkins Micawber, based rather closely on Dickens' own father, is both weak and theatrical—a one-man show acutely aware of his persona and incapable of saying anything that has not been burnished for dramatic effect.

For Micawber, language itself is a mask: it conceals his chronically shabby state. Micawber is, according to his own script, "a man of some experience in life" who despite certain limitations and an unending flow of bad luck, has "surmounted difficulties and conquered obstacles" while gathering up insights that are the keys to a successful life. "Procrastination is the thief of time," he lectures David. "Collar him!"

Micawber's wife, Emma, clearly learned long ago to take a part in her husband's continuous production; by doing so she earns a certain nobility while distracting herself from buried resentments that have a way of bubbling up. Speaking with David, Mrs. Micawber admits that her husband is "improvident"; that he "concealed his difficulties from me in the first instance"; that he pawned her jewelry, "inherited from mamma," for "less than half their value"; that he has been an endless source of tension between herself and her family. And yet she presents herself as a rock of fidelity and proclaims her virtue in the stagy, overdone style of someone less interested in convincing others than in convincing herself. "He is the parent of my children! He is the father of my twins! He is the husband of my affections. And I ne-ver-will-desert Mr. Micawber!"

David is a rather passive figure, and as he tries to find himself he takes on an assortment of names, identities and roles. His idol James Steerforth—who masks his own insecurities with a bravado performance as the smooth young man-about town—calls David "Daisy," old school slang for an effeminate man.

Not surprisingly, then, when David falls in love with Dora he has picked a young woman who is both similar to his late mother (a self-described "weak, light, girlish figure") and as ill-defined as himself. Dora has been spoiled by an indulged upbringing in a sheltered home. She has no real notion of adulthood or of real life, but the part she plays—the empty-headed little flirt—has so far won good reviews. When it becomes clear to David (and Dora herself) that the part is getting stale, she grows anxious, begging David to stick to the script. Call me "child-wife," she directs him; "you should think of me that way. When you are going to be angry with me, say to yourself it's only my child-wife!"

Uriah Heep is also repeating a role he learned many years before. Heep's late father gave him this acting tip: "'People like to be above you, keep yourself down.'" This rule was enforced at the "charitable" school Uriah attended: "They taught us all a good deal of umbleness.—not much else that I know of, from morning to night. We was to be umble to this person, and umble to that; and to pull off our caps here, and to make bows there; and ways to know our place, and abase ourselves before our betters. And we had such a lot of betters!" Heep's father played the part so well, "among the gentlefolks," that they made him a sexton—steady work, that. "Be umble,' says father, 'and you'll do!" Heep seethes in the part, but he can no more shed it than he can shed his own skin. He can only keep bowing and cringing and wringing his hands even as he secretly connives to best his betters and finally get what he craves.

David detests Heep, particularly when he discovers that what this "malevolent baboon" really craves is the estimable Agnes Wickfield. And yet, in some ways, the two characters are quite alike: Heep is David's ugly twin. They are both fatherless young men making their way in an unforgiving world. They must lift themselves or be lost.

1849-50

David studies shorthand; Heep crams law. And they both love, and very much need, Agnes Wickfield—a fact Heep grasps more readily than David himself.

The novel pairs other characters in a similar way. Agnes' father, Mr. Wickfield, a well-plumed lawyer, would seem to have little in common with Mrs. Gummidge, the "lone lorn creetur" who keeps house for Daniel Peggotty. But both have lost a spouse, and both stew in a state of mourning grown morbid with time. Wickfield, of course, comes to realize that his grieving and his drinking have made him vulnerable to the dark schemes of Heep, who—as the novel repeatedly hints—has the more primal instincts of an animal, knowing when to strike and when to retreat. "Weak indulgence has ruined me," moans Mr. Wickfield. "Indulgence in remembrance, and indulgence in forgetfulness. My natural grief for my child's mother turned to disease; my natural love for my child turned to disease. I have infected everything I touched. I have preyed on my own morbid coward heart, and it has preyed on me."

Heep, who sees right through David, taunts him on his choice of Dora: "You have sometimes plucked a pear before it was ripe, Master Copperfield?" And in fact, David and Dora cannot hope to function in the world as such a weak and flighty pair. The housekeepers they hire quickly smell this weakness and grow lax themselves. However unintentionally, "we are positively corrupting people," David tells Dora, in words that echo Mr. Wickfield's. "It is a reflection I am unable to dismiss, and sometimes it makes me very uneasy."

He's uneasy because, as *David Copperfield* shows, only truly strong people can hope to get through life on terms of their own. Weak people (Mr. Dick, Mr. Wickfield, Mr. Micawber and the distracted, ironically named Dr. Strong) must rely on others in order to survive. Or else—like Dora and Steerforth and Clara Copperfield—they end up dead. Notably, the weak characters in *David Copperfield* are mostly male. Although Micawber and David try to convince themselves otherwise, both are in varying ways deluded and best at building castles in the air. Poor Mr. Dick, who frankly and happily calls himself weak, is a grown man with the emotions of a child.

In *David Copperfield*, with the vivid exception of that stalwart seaman, Mr. Peggotty, the strongest characters are women. Peggotty's sister Clara, young David's nurse, is both gentle and robust, a good-hearted woman with good strong arms. Agnes Wickfield, a pillar of calm resolve, keeps her father on the rails before saving David too. Aunt Betsey is magnificently eccentric, but she is also the soundest character in the book—a real adult who knows all about the hardness of life and the vagaries of human character and who girds herself accordingly. Aunt Betsey guides David, boosts and shelters Mr. Dick, and bails out Micawber. She is a shrewd judge of character and a reliable dispenser of sound advice. She is self-reflective, it turns out; but she is also generous, compassionate, and immune to intimidation. She has "useful possession of her wits," as David observes.

It's no wonder she wanted Clara Copperfield's first baby to be a girl.

Dickens
Down Under

....

Australia fascinated Dickens. Over the years, in moments of weariness or exasperation, he would sometimes muse about starting over down under, or at least touring there lucratively with his literary one-man show. "I think all the probabilities for such a country as Australia," Dickens told Forster, "are immense."

Dickens never did get to Australia. But he did send several characters there. In *David Copperfield*, Wilkins Micawber moves with his family to Australia, where—we're told—this conspicuous English failure finally makes his mark. The disgraced Little Emily also gets a fresh start far away, as did some of the women who, in real life, sheltered at Urania Cottage, the home for reforming prostitutes that Dickens and Angela Burdett-Coutts had established in Shepherd's Bush. Dickens' magazine *Household Words* actively supported the idea of British immigration to the colonies, particularly Australia, where stable families and marriageable women were, for some years, in short supply.

From the start, *Household Words* took close note of Australia, its landscape and history. Many émigrés, the magazine noted, looked for a fresh start, a new challenge; others hoped to dig for gold. An 1853 article, "First Stage to Australia," observed the "stream of fustian jackets, corduroy trousers and smock-frocks, the chattering excited parties of half-shaven mechanics, slatternly females, and slip-shod children"—the clamor of the crowds that gathered at the Colonial Land and Emigration Commission in Park Street, where busy bureaucrats filled forms and added numbers and decided, finally, who could leave for Australia and who could not. At that time, "blacksmiths, carpenters, sawyers, gardeners, agriculturists, with their wives and families" were given preference. Butchers, bakers, tailors, green-grocers and "single men" generally were not.

Other articles in *Household Words* chronicled the history of the Australian continent, or surveyed its exotic animal life. In "Four Legged Australians" (1853) Samuel Rinder describes the wombat, the "native Devil" (a "very ugly, very savage brute"), the Flying Squirrel (whose "bright eyes are set in two circles of deep black, which give a very arch expression to the face") and the "darkly, deeply, beautifully Blue Kangaroo—found only in the colonies of Swan River and South Australia."

But getting there was a trial, as Dickens' magazines made clear. "A Digger's Diary" (Richard Horne's account, in "occasional chapters") recounts a long crossing during which, somewhere near Madeira, the ship's cooks discovered that much of the tinned food had spoiled, emitting "the most disgusting fumes imaginable." The provisions were tossed overboard, much to the disgust of the ship's captain, who was blunt in his blame: "'That's a sad waste of provisions; Mssrs. Saltash and Pincher had better have paid a trifle more to the contractors. Penny wise and pound foolish.'" Implicit in many of  these Australian pieces is the belief that progress—in Australia and elsewhere—was being impeded by the short-sighted practices of businessmen and government officials obsessed with making their large profit and nothing more.

In fact, the ship was hazardous, as Horne recounts. Shipmates frequently fell overboard, where they were found by sharks: "I looked over the side, and was just in time to see the sailor, with a face as white as a ghost, swung backwards and disappear beneath the wave. His mouth was wide open—I think with horror—some said he gave a scream, but I never heard it." Children too were in danger. Two boys died when, playing, they "fell down the fore hatchway, and down through the open hatchway of the hold." "The babes had been murdered," their distraught mothers cried, "by the want of proper protection and fenders."

Another piece, "Canvass Town," showed the difficulties that awaited immigrants once they arrived. The author, Horne, calls himself "the youngest son of a landed proprietor in Essex," and records the ordeal of landing with his wife and children in Melbourne, where too many people were left looking for too few accommodations. But mosquitoes and fleas were plentiful in the packed boarding houses: "In the morning every part of every one of us was covered with red swellings, or small red punctures. My eldest daughter, eight years of age, was a speckled blight, and my wife's under lip was a tomato." The author takes shelter in a zone of some six hundred tents—the "canvass town" where, for weeks, families were forced to settle down while they search for permanent shelter and work.

At one point, the author finds himself selling most of his belongings at "a strip of waste ground near the wharf, which was called Rag Fair. I was even obliged to consent, on one or two occasions, when I was unwell from exposure to the heat, to allow my wife to go there and to take her stand behind an open box, with its contents spread out on the ground in front and around it, waiting for purchasers. Strange and sad work for a baronet's daughter!"

The Distant Shore

Life's a fight, as Dickens knew—perhaps particularly for immigrants settling the new colonies, and for those the colonists displaced. The author of "Bungaree, King of the Blacks," an 1859 essay in *All the Year Round*, recalls his long friendship with an older aboriginal man for whom the arrival of the colonists had meant nothing but death and decline. King Bungaree, as he called himself, had become a fixture in Sydney, something of a comical figure in a cocked-hat and cast-off military coat. But the author sees what's behind the intoxicated charade. Bungaree had once been a respected figure in his tribe—a strong, vital man. Now he was a pitiable beggar, the victim of malice and scorn. The author asks Bungaree about one of his wives, and learns: "'Two emigrant mans get drunk and kill her with brickbat on top o'rocks.'"

Bungaree and his people, the author declares, "had been contaminated and corrupted by their more civilized fellow-creatures, and their whole thoughts seemed to be centered in how they could most speedily become intoxicated and sleep off its effects." Bungaree, notes the author, "was the only old aboriginal I ever saw in the vicinity of Sydney. Drink, and its effects, destroyed the majority of both sexes long before they attained the prime of life."

For the restless Dickens, the idea of emigration never quite lost its appeal. During the 1860s, he urged two of his sons, Alfred and Edward, to seek opportunities in New South Wales. For a time, both sons prospered in Australia; Edward served in Parliament from 1889 to 1894. They benefitted from their father's estate; they did not, however inherit his financial skills. They were "improvident" as Mrs. Micawber might say. But Alfred, later in life, did enjoy renewed success by lecturing widely on his father's life and work in Europe and in the United States.

ALL IN A NAME

In his *Life of Charles Dickens*, John Forster offers a glimpse of the author's working papers, including lists of some of the names Dickens generated for possible use. These include:

Towndling.	Tertius Jobber.	Holblack.	Brankle.
Mood.	Amon	Mulley.	Mag.
Guff.	Headston.	Redworth.	Chellyson.
Treble.	Strayshott.	Redfoot.	Blenham—Cl.
Chilby.	Higden.	Tarbox (B).	Bardock.
Spessifer.	Morfit.	Tinkling.	Snigsworth.
Sittern.	Goldstraw.	Duddle.	Swenton.
Dostone.	Wodder.	Jebus.	Casby—Beach.
Cay-lon.	Whelpford.	Powderhill.	Lowleigh—
Snowell.	Fennerck.	Grimmer.	Lowely.
Lottrum.	Gannerson.	Skuse.	Pigrin.
Lammle.	Chinkerble.	Titcoombe.	Yerbury.
Frosser.	Bintrey.	Crabble.	Plornish.
Slyvant.	Wozenham.	Fledson.	Maroon.
Queedy.	Stiltwalk.	Hirll.	Bandy-Nandy.
Besselthur.	Stiltingstalk.	Brayle.	Stonebury.
Musty.	Stiltstalking.	Mullender.	Magwitch.
Grout.	Ravendar.	Treslingham.	Meagles.

CAPSULE

BLEAK HOUSE.

1852-53

In 1851, when Dickens began *Bleak House*, the influence of lawyers and the courts was a topic of growing public interest and ethical concern. In both Britain and the United States, there was "a vague popular belief that lawyers are necessarily dishonest," wrote one American lawyer, Abraham Lincoln, around 1850; in fact the "impression of dishonesty is very distinct and vivid," almost "universal." Lincoln urged his fellow lawyers never to "stir up litigation," nor take large fees in advance of settlement.

Above all, "discourage litigation. Persuade your neighbors to compromise whenever you can. Point out to them how the nominal winner is often a real loser—in fees, and expenses, and waste of time. As a peace maker the lawyer has superior opertunity [sic] of being a good man. There will still be business enough."

The lawyers in *Bleak House* never received Lincoln's memo. They exploit a case—Jarndyce and Jarndyce—that involves a disputed will and has lingered in the Court of Chancery for many years. Its resolution obsesses many of the novel's key characters—some rich, some poor; some hiding secrets and others obsessed with digging those secrets out.

Here the law is "nothing but fees, fraud, horsehair wigs and black gowns." It's a corrupt, self-promoting cult. "The great principle of Eng-lish law," *Bleak House* asserts, "is to make business for itself." Thus, "it becomes a coherent scheme, and not the monstrous maze the laity are apt to think it. Let them but once clearly perceive that its grand principle is to make business for itself at their expense, and surely they will cease to grumble."

The unctuous, rodent-like Vholes squeezes fees from hapless clients as he congratulates himself on his tireless support of his family. The black-clad Tulkinghorn is reputed to have made "good thrift out of aristocratic marriage settlements and aristocratic wills, and to be very rich." Tulkinghorn is sullen, aloof, "an oyster of the old school whom nobody can open." He lives in a large house in Lincoln's Inn Fields, where lawyers "lie like maggots in nuts."

In *Bleak House*, extreme self-regard is a central theme. In an 1853 essay, Dickens writes: "Egotism is one of the most offensive and contemptible littlenesses a civilized man can exhibit, so it is really incompatible with the interchange of ideas; in as much as if we all talked about ourselves we should soon have no listeners, and must be yelling and screeching at once on our own separate accounts: making society hideous."

Several characters are blinded by their self-preoccupations and pride. Harold Skimpole is a sponger who—

like "the begging-letter writers" Dickens so despised—also thinks mainly of the sums he can extract from the gullible and kind. "I dare say I owe as much as good-natured people will let me owe . If they don't stop, why should I?" Mrs. Jellyby, meanwhile, pursues her charitable efforts for far-flung causes with a "superior air" and with little regard for own family. She takes her dishevelment as a source of pride. Her house is a tip and her hair looks like "the mane of a dustman's horse."

The haughty Sir Leicester Dedlock is a bit more likable; still, he symbolizes the useless, decaying aristocracy that Dickens often condemns, and he presides over a stuffy estate that, Dickens implies, will soon give way to the modern world. Leicester supports parasitic "cousins" who "lounge in purposeless and listless paths, and seem to be quite as much at a loss how to dispose of themselves, as anybody else can be how to dispose of them."

Dedlock's wife Honoria is "beautiful, elegant, accomplished." But it's Lady Dedlock's secret that especially intrigues Tulkinghorn and other unsavory characters, including Krook, the shabby shop owner who is consumed by the raging forces of spontaneous combustion.

Bleak House is part Samuel Beckett, part Upton Sinclair. The words of Skimpole, Matthew Bagnet, "Mr. George," and William Guppy are comically absurd. The Smallweeds are marvelous grotesques. There's humor too in certain scenes with Mr. Inspector Bucket—a proto-Lieutenant Columbo

who owes much to Charles F. Field, a member of the Metropolitan Constabulary. Dickens liked Field, and featured him in several articles written in praise of London's diligent police. Jo, the young street sweeper, is also sympathetically drawn, and his presence links *Bleak House* thematically to *Oliver Twist* and *A Christmas Carol*. In *Bleak House* smug rich people prey and hoard while, around them, filth mounts, disease festers, and children starve.

Other sympathetic characters include John Jardnyce, who is wealthy but unconcerned with wealth and who bestows, on his housekeeper Esther Summerson, his selfless love and goodwill. Esther, who narrates much of *Bleak House*, is quietly generous and tough, overcoming a desolate childhood and a later bout with smallpox with stoic good cheer. She gains a suitable marriage to the "sensible" Allan Woodcourt, a selfless physician who—unlike all those disagreeable lawyers—will actually do some good in the world.

"We are not rich in the bank," Esther explains, "but we have always prospered, and we have quite enough. I never walk out with my husband, but I hear people bless him." "I never lie down at night, but I know that in the course of that day he has alleviated pain, and soothed some fellow-creature in the time of need. I know that from the beds of those who were past recovery, thanks have often, often gone up, in the last hour, for his patient ministration. Is not this to be rich?"

COULD IT HAPPEN TO YOU?

LONDON MAN DIES IN MYSTERY FIRE

In *Bleak House* the character of Krook comes to a famously bad end. Krook keeps a cluttered shop and lets rooms near Lincoln's Inn. He is a "short, cadaverous, and withered" figure, not given to social niceties, and he wears a "hairy cap and coat." He is "continually in liquor," we're told—an entirely charmless, crooked man who sells cat's skins, among other things. And one night his body—or rather, what's left of it—is found near his usual chair, in his dingy shop, where, oddly, "there is a smouldering suffocating vapour in the room, and a dark greasy coating on the ceiling."

Krook has dissolved, somehow, left to resemble a "broken log of wood sprinkled with white ashes." He's the victim, we're told, of "Spontaneous Combustion," a rare but verifiable form of demise that is "inborn, inbred, engendered in the corrupted humours of the vicious body itself."

Readers replied. George Lewes, who often wrote about scientific subjects for a general audience, suggested that Dickens' description of Krook's death was based on nothing remotely resembling fact, but was probably inspired by his friend Captain Marryat, the popular novelist who had once dispatched a character through similar means. Dickens, Lewes argued, could never find "an organic chemist of any authority" to believe that the human body, composed mainly of water, could just suddenly burst into flames. If you believe this, Lewes wrote, you might also believe that gunpowder could ignite if mixed with three times its own weight of water." Dickens' genius was mani-

Up in smoke

fest "in so many other directions than that of Physiology," Lewes observed. "It would cost you nothing," he urged the novelist, "to avow a mistake."

Dickens admitted that *Bleak House* had "purposely dwelt upon the romantic side of familiar things." But he also stressed, in a later preface to the novel, that "I do not willfully or negligently mislead my readers." He "took pains" to investigate the phenomena of spontaneous combustion before describing Krook's death.

In his preface, and in a separate reply to Lewes, Dickens summarized his findings: there were at least "thirty cases on record, of which the most famous, that of the Countess Cornelia de Baudi Cesenate, was investigated and described by Giuseppe Bianchini, a prebendary of Verona, otherwise distinguished in letters, who published an account of it at Verona in 1731, which he afterwards published at Rome." Another case, perhaps less glamorous, but no less convincing to Dickens, was "very clearly described" by no less an authority than a dentist from Ohio. It "occurred at the town of Columbus, in the United States of America, quite recently. The subject was a German who kept a liquor-shop and was an inveterate drunkard."

According to Dickens, heavy drinkers were, in fact, far more likely to self-ignite. He pointed to other cited examples, including "Mary Clues—a woman of fifty and a drunkard," and Grace Pitt—a woman of sixty: not stated to be a drunkard, but not likely to have been a lady of very temperate habits, as she got out of bed every night to smoke a pipe, and

113

had drunk an immense quantity of spirits within a few hours of her death."

Reports of spontaneous combustion do continue to occur. Haystacks, farmers know, can sometimes catch fire—the result of bacteria activated in the core of bales that have been drenched by rain and then scorched by heat. Other substances—coal, finely powdered ores—are also linked under certain circumstances to spontaneous combustion.

Certainly, spontaneous human combustion—or SHC as some researchers prefer to call it—remains an intriguing topic for cable television shows and books bearing titles like *Fires From Heaven* and *The Entrancing Flame*. One often-cited case involved the Florida woman who, back in the 1950s, was found in a smoldering heap in her favorite chair—even though the room around her, as well as her slippered foot, appeared to be largely untouched by fire or smoke. In other, similar cases, the knees and lower legs are left intact, while the rest of the body is left as a fine white powder.

In the late 1970s, police in Wales encountered a similar scene when they entered a house and—according to newspaper accounts—were struck in the main room by "a yeasty smell" and a strange, orange-red glow. They found no fire, only heat, and walls "coated in a glutinous substance," as if the room had been turned into "the inside of an oven, where meat has been regularly roasted." And there on the floor: "a pair of human feet in socks and attached to the lower portion of a body."

According to another, more recent account, a man traveling by car through Hungary stopped momentarily to urinate near the side of the road. Suddenly he was surrounded, reported his companion, by a vivid, glowing blue light. Incongruously, according to this report, a bus carrying physicians from a nearby conference just happened to pass by, but no one could save the man who had inexplicably burned alive. A later autopsy, goes the story, revealed that the man's internal organs had been incinerated into carbon.

Theories abound. "Drunkards" are no longer deemed prime victims; instead, argue some theorists, SHC—like spontaneous combustion in hay—stems from bacteria, rapidly multiplying. Others cite unusually high levels of methane, or static electricity. Still others blame sun flares that effect the earth's magnetic field and prompt dangerous "discharges" inside the body. And yet another expert in the field contends, not yet to wide avail, that spontaneous combustion derives from "an internal subatomic chain reaction" caused by "subatomic particles called pyrotrons."

Sceptics, however, have suggested that when a man burns up in his easy chair the cause is perhaps less likely to be solar flares than, say, flammable pajamas and a dropped cigar. Other experiments have shown that the well-known hallmarks of SHC probably owe not to some raging internal combustion, but to the "candle effect." In this theory clothing that has caught fire functions as a wick, igniting the body's fat, which adds fuel to the flames. Under certain conditions, liquefied human fat can burn intensely in a highly concentrated way, leaving behind the piles of white ash and the greasy soot that poor Guppy found when, on that bleak London night, he came upon Krook's charred remains.

Still, some well-known writers continue to stand with Dickens, not Lewes. The late Arthur C. Clarke, for example, intrigued by a variety of modern cases, refused to dismiss the possibility of Spontaneous Human Combustion. Colin Wilson, looking at similar evidence, was no less convinced than Dickens by what he found. "Only an idiot," wrote Wilson, "could remain unconvinced." "Far from being a myth, spontaneous combustion," he declared, "is a horrifying reality."

Dickens On Education

❝ Mere reading and writing is not education; it would be quite as reasonable to call bricks and mortar architecture—oils and colours art—reeds and cat-gut music—or the child's spelling-books the works of Shakespeare, Milton, or Bacon—as to call the lowest rudiments of education, education, and to visit on that most abused and slandered word their failure in any instance; and precisely because they were not education; because, generally speaking, the word has been understood in that sense a great deal too long; because education for the business of life, and for the due cultivation of domestic virtues, is at least as important from day to day to the grown person as to the child; because real education, in the strife and contention for a livelihood, and the consequent necessity incumbent on a great number of young persons to go into the world when they are very young, is extremely difficult. It is because of these things that I look upon mechanics' institutions and athenæums as vitally important to the well-being of society. It is because the rudiments of education may there be turned to good account in the acquisition of sound principles, and of the great virtues, hope, faith, and charity, to which all our knowledge tends; it is because of that, I take it, that you have met in education's name to-night. ❞

—Charles Dickens, speaking at the opening of The Glasgow Athenæum, December 28, 1847.

DICKENS ON SANITATION

❝ Of what avail is it to send missionaries to the miserable man condemned to work in a fœtid court, with every sense bestowed upon him for his health and happiness turned into a torment, with every month of his life adding to the heap of evils under which he is condemned to exist? What human sympathy within him is that instructor to address? What natural old chord within him is he to touch? Is it the remembrance of his children?—a memory of destitution, of sickness, of fever, and of scrofula? Is it his hopes, his latent hopes of immortality? He is so surrounded by and embedded in material filth, that his soul cannot rise to the contemplation of the great truths of religion. Or if the case is that of a miserable child bred and nurtured in some noisome, loathsome place, and tempted, in these better days, into the ragged school, what can a few hours' teaching effect against the ever-renewed lesson of a whole existence? But give them a glimpse of heaven through a little of its light and air; give them water; help them to be clean; lighten that heavy atmosphere in which their spirits flag and in which they become the callous things they are … and then they will be brought willingly to hear of Him whose thoughts were so much with the poor, and who had compassion for all human suffering. **❞**

—Charles Dickens, speaking at a meeting of the Metropolitan Sanitary Association, May 10, 1851.

CAPSULE

HARD TIMES.

1854

Hard Times, the first Dickens novel to be serialized in *Household Words*, is dedicated to Thomas Carlyle, whose social criticism was widely admired during much of Queen Victoria's reign. Carlyle was a complex, often controversial thinker, and Dickens didn't agree with everything he had to say. But Dickens did admire his erudition and his blazing if perhaps idiosyncratic intellectual energy. And he certainly accepted Carlyle's critique of the deadening forces of materialism that, in Carlyle's view, were re-defining British society.

Carlyle condemned "the Mammon-Gospel" and its bleak creed based on greed. It was the age of money, Carlyle complained, a time of wide hoarding and crass pursuits. It was "the Age of Machinery" too, "in every outward and inward sense of the word; the age which, with its whole undivided might, forwards, teaches and practices the great art of adapting means to ends." It was "the domain of Mechanism" in which utilitarian values ruled.

But Man of course is more than Mechanical. From his "Dynamical nature" come "the mysterious springs of Love, and Fear, and Wonder, of Enthusiasm, Poetry, Religion, all which have a truly vital and infinite character." "If we read History with any degree of thoughtfulness," Carlyle wrote, "we shall find that the checks and balances of Profit and Loss have never been the grand agents with men; that they have never been roused into deep, thorough, all-pervading efforts by any computable prospect of Profit and Loss, for any visible, finite object; but always for some invisible and infinite one."

John Ruskin, no less influential, had similar concerns. Ruskin's *The Stones of Venice* (1853) also criticized the rise of utilitarian values—the assumption, for example, that workers were merely tools. "We have much studied and much perfected, of late, the great civilized invention of the division of labor," Ruskin observed, "only we give it a false name. It is not, truly speaking, the labor that is divided, but the men—divided into mere segments of men—broken into small fragments and crumbs of life."

See, thus, the workers in a bead factory who "sit at their work all day, their hands vibrating with a perpetual and exquisitely timed palsy, and the beads dropping beneath their vibration like hail." "In all of our manufacturing cities, we manufacture everything there except men; we blanch cotton, and strengthen steel, and refine sugar, and shape pottery; but to brighten, to strength, to refine, or to form a single living spirit, never enters into our estimate of advantages."

Hard Times is much informed by such views. It's set in Coketown, a place of dreary factories and relentless work.

Stephen Blackpool is, for Dickens, a representative working man, underpaid and undervalued, constrained on all sides. He is harried by union organizers who want him to join the fight for labourer's rights. In *Hard Times* and elsewhere, Dickens tends to depict working people with sympathy as well as sentimentality; he is wary, however, of wide and lasting social reform ever coming up from their ranks. Thus the "cunning" Slackbridge, with his "sour expression" and "lowering brows" is a highly unappealing leader of the worker's revolt; like Bounderby, he'll happily smash anyone who blocks his path.

Blackpool's other antagonist is Josiah Bounderby—industrialist, bank owner, and monstrous champion of the Mammon Gospel. Bounderby is the creation of a writer who specialized in comically grotesque figures, from the bloated, blue-faced Major Bagstock in *Dombey and Son* to the pious hypocrite Chadband in *Bleak House*, "a large yellow man, with a fat smile, and a general appearance of having a good deal of train oil in his system." Here is a writer who, as a boy, was both fascinated and frightened by the scary puppets and masks of the kind made by the mean Tackleton in *The Cricket on the Hearth*. Bounderby, in fact, appears to be "made out of a coarse material, which seemed to have stretched to make so much of him." He has "a great puffed head" with bulging veins in his temples. He is "a man with a pervading appearance on him of being inflated like a balloon, and ready to start." His stare is stony and he has a "metallic" laugh.

Coketown is dreadful, an unheavenly city where men and women work unrelentingly, like machines, finding occasional refreshment when, for example, Mister Sleary's ragtag Circus comes to town. Coketown is a "triumph of fact," run by men with no idea of beauty and no sense of play. It has "a black canal in it, and a river with ill-smelling dye." It has streets "all very like one another, inhabited by people equally like one another, who all went in at the same hours, with the same sound upon the pavements, to do the same work, and to whom every day was the same as yesterday and tomorrow, and every year the counterpart of the last and the next." Everything in Coketown is functional, monotonous, "workful." "The jail might have been the infirmity, the infirmity might have been the jail, the town-hall might have been either, or both."

Thomas Gradgrind, the local schoolmaster, shows what happens when a mediocre, unimaginative mind decides that utilitarianism is the key to successful living. As Dickens was regularly revealing in *Household Words*, the world brimmed with fascinating things: strange animals, exotic cultures, momentous scientific discoveries. But at Gradgrind's school bullying and parrot-learning are the order of the day. Gradgrind treats his students—even his own children, Tom and Louisa—like programmable machines.

The results prove unfortunate. Tom grows selfish. Louisa pleases her father by marrying Bounderby, the least attractive husband since Daniel Quilp. Finally she confronts the thick

1854

Gradgrind: "How could you give me life, and take from me all the inappreciable things that raise it from conscious death?" "Where," she demands—using words that Estella will similarly hurl at her oppressor, Miss Havisham—"are the graces of my soul? Where are the sentiments of my heart?" Louisa, striking her breast, demands: "What have you done, with the garden that should have bloomed once, in this great wilderness here!" Louisa is dynamic but made mechanical—all those "mysterious springs" that Carlyle describes have gone dry.

Dickens, one thinks, is also defending himself in *Hard Times*, implicitly arguing against those critics who repeatedly lectured him on the implausibility of his characters and plots; who, like George Lewes for example, had scolded him for presenting a death by "spontaneous combustion" and ignoring the relevant scientific "facts."

Some critics did call *Hard Times* over-the-top—another Dickensian tour of a bizarre world no normal person could recognize. *Hard Times*, observed the *Westminster Review*, aims to "exhibit the evil effects of an exclusive education of the intellect, without a due cultivation of the finer feelings of the heart and fancy." But where, the journal's reviewer wondered, did such places actually exist?

"We are not aware of such a system being in operation anywhere in England. On the contrary, it is the opinion of various continental professors, very competent to form a judgment on this subject, that more play is given to the imagination and will by the English system of instruction than by any other."

In fact, "if we look to our public schools and universities, we find great part, too great part, we think, of the period of youth and adolescence devoted to the study of the mythology, literature, and history of the most poetic people of all time." In almost "every school in the kingdom, passages of our finest poets are learned by heart; and Shakespeare and Walter Scott are among the Penates of every decent family. If there are Gradgrind schools, they are not sufficiently numerous to be generally known."

And who, really, wants to read about such characters, or enter their "cold and uncongenial atmosphere?" "One can have no more pleasure in being present at this compression and disfigurement than in witnessing the application of the boot—nor in following these poor souls, thus intellectually halt and maimed, through life, than in seeing Chinese ladies hobbling through a race."

For this literal-minded reviewer, *Hard Times* didn't offer a sufficient number of recognizable characters "less repulsive than the Gradgrinds, Bounderbys" and more representative of the nation's many earnest educators and their "practicable" plans. But then, lamented the *Westminster Review*, what can one expect from the talented Charles Dickens these days? Invariably, his most successful characters "are the simplest and lest cultivated." The others, "even when they are only of the bourgeois class, are nearly always furnished with some peculiarity, which, like the weight of a Dutch clock, is their ever-gravitating principle of action." Such characters and their absurd doings "may excite a laugh, perhaps, in a farce spoken at the Victoria, but will hardly do so with any reader of taste."

Now Mr. Thackeray, the reviewer suggests, would never write such a preposterous book. But then, Mr. Thackeray has "the most intimate acquaintance with human nature of any novel writer of the day." He'd never construct a "puppet" like Bounderby, "a most outrageous character—who can believe in the possibility of such a man?"

Charlie Chaplin for one. Chaplin, Dickensian in so many ways, may have been thinking of *Hard Times* when he wrote the famous anti-fascism speech that comes near the close of *The Great Dictator*, his satire of Hitler's Germany. Playing the modest barber who, mistaken for the dictator, addresses a crowd accustomed to ugly rants, Chaplin delivers words that could easily have been Dickens' own. Someday, hopes Chaplin's character, "science and progress" will bring happiness to all mankind.

But before then we must face the hard facts: "greed has poisoned men's souls." "Machinery that has given abundance has left us in want." We are led by "machine men with machine hearts." "More than machinery, we need humanity." "We think too much and feel too little." Without governing systems that are devoted to humanity as well as efficiency and power, "life will be violent, and all will be lost."

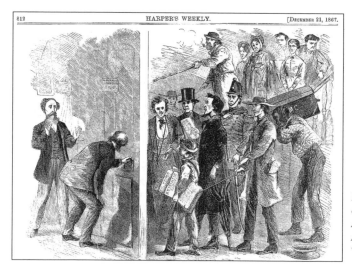

812　　　　　　　HARPER'S WEEKLY.　　　　[DECEMBER 21, 1867.

Mr. Charles Dickens and his former American Acquaintances-- "Not at Home"

John Ruskin on Charles Dickens

" The essential value and truth of Dickens' writings have been unwisely lost sight of by many thoughtful persons, merely because he presents his truth with some colour of caricature. Unwisely, because Dickens' caricature, though often gross, is never mistaken. Allowing for his manner of telling them, the things he tells us are always true. I wish that he could think it right to limit his brilliant exaggeration to works written only for public amusement; and when he takes up a subject of high national importance, such as that which he handled in *Hard Times*, that he would use severer and more accurate analysis. ... But let us not lose the use of Dickens' wit and insight, because he chooses to speak in a circle of stage fire. He is entirely right in his main drift and purpose in every book he has written; and all of them, but especially *Hard Times*, should be studied with close and earnest care by persons interested in social questions. **"**

The Top of the Tree:
Dickens vs. Thackeray

....

"In the literary period I know best," writes John Sutherland, "the 19th century, I have always believed that readers divide into two great taste sectors: Thackerayans, who like fiction which talks, conversationally to them; and Dickensians, who like their fiction to be theatrical: a spectacle at which they are spectators. One can, of course, appreciate both *Vanity Fair* and *Dombey and Son*, as demonstrably many cultivated Victorians did in 1848, when both novels first appeared in monthly serial form. But my guess is that most readers will, in their novel-reading hearts, have had a fond preference for one author's method over the others."

Many Victorian critics and readers probably did assume that Dickens and Thackeray were, in fact, keen rivals who carefully measured each other's influence and fame. Thackeray was generally considered the more intellectual of the two, the more artistically refined. The great essayist Thomas Huxley, for example, much preferred Thackeray's autobiographical novel *Pendennis* to Dickens' *David Copperfield*. Dickens, wrote Huxley, is "not a great artist and rarely dips much below the surface." But *Pendennis* caught "more nearly than any book I know" the condition of "thirsting" young men "fighting their way up."

Dickens and Thackeray were actually on very cordial terms—at least most of the time. They shared many of the same friends, moved in similar social and literary circles, and were both satirists at heart. Thackeray and his children were frequent guests in Dickens' home; their daughters were for years close friends. But one senses that, just below the surface, sharp tensions had always informed Dickens' friendship with Thackeray: they liked each other as true competitors often do—warily. And they were separated by a wide range of assumptions and values based, at least partly, on class.

In age, they were only a year apart. But Thackeray enjoyed early opportunities that the young Dickens could only read about in books. Thackeray was born in Calcutta, where his father held a high post in the British East India Company. Thackeray grew up in wealthy surroundings and attended prestigious boarding schools in Britain. Although his father died when Thackeray was around five, his mother remarried well, and—around the time Dickens was teaching himself shorthand and reading library books—Thackeray was sent to Trinity College, Cambridge, where he lodged near Isaac Newton's old rooms. Thackeray, though, wasn't much inspired by his academic surroundings. He quickly fell in with a fast set, took up gambling, ignored his studies, and left without a degree.

It wasn't a complete catastrophe. Thackeray's stepfather helped bankroll his tour of the continent, and bought him a commission in the Devon Yeomanry. Thus, while Dickens was rubbing elbows with impoverished clerks—the William Guppys and Dick Swivellers of the world—Thackeray was swanning about France and Germany in a military uniform, visiting salons, chatting with Goethe, attending the opera, playing cards and, not incidentally, gathering a good deal of material he would later use in *Vanity Fair*.

Thackeray's life turned Dickensian when, in 1833, he found himself quite broke, and with no means of familial support. By the time they reached their late twenties, Dickens was famous and Thackeray was trying desperately to make his name as an illustrator or a writer—sketching and scribbling away to pay his bills. Quietly, Dickens may have despised the way Thackeray squandered his youthful opportunities. He clearly didn't like the way in which Thackeray (despite his own keen nose for snobbism in all its forms) seemed always to court the company of so many second-rate barons and earls.

And Thackeray, it seems, rather resented Dickens' vast success. He made much of their supposed rivalry, noting in one letter that, thanks to the success of *Vanity Fair*, he was "all but at the top of the tree," and "having a great fight up there with Dickens." For Thackeray, too many things about Dickens—his public moral earnestness, his undignified theatrical barnstorming— were not becoming in a true gentleman of letters.

Well-known as a sly mocker of his other literary rivals (including Harrison Ainsworth and Edward Bulwer-Lytton), Thackeray did not make a point of attacking Dickens in print (although, in an early piece for *Fraser's Magazine*, he complained that "Boz, who knows life well," should have resisted his sentimentalized portrait of a prostitute in *Oliver Twist*; for "his Miss Nancy is the most unreal fantastical personage possible; no more like a thief's mistress than one of Gesner's shepherdesses resembles a real country wench.") Instead Thackeray admitted that his own daughters were very loyal Dickens readers; one of them "when she is happy, reads *Nicholas Nickleby*; when she is unhappy, reads *Nicholas Nickleby*; when she is in bed, reads *Nicholas Nickleby*; when she has nothing to do, reads *Nicholas Nickleby*; and when she has finished the book, reads *Nicholas Nickleby* over again." "Lucky is he," wrote Thackeray, with perhaps only a touch of condescension, "who has such a charming gift of nature as this, which brings all the children in the world trooping to him, and being fond of him."

But sometimes in his private writings a barbed edge—a hint of envy—pokes through. Once, in 1849, Thackeray spotted Dickens and his family at Ryde, returning from a holiday on the Isle of Wight. Thackeray's own family life was shadowed by the chronic mental illness of his wife, and he apparently sometimes assumed that Dickens, like Bob Cratchit, presided over a warm and cheery household. There, on the pier, Thackeray wrote, was "the great Dickens with his wife his children his Miss Hogarth all looking abominably coarse vulgar and happy."

In 1857, Dickens, some assumed, had Thackeray in mind

when he created Henry Gowan, the snobbish and feckless artist who marries Minnie Meagles in *Little Dorrit*. Gowan had inherited "a small independence," but "his genius, during his earlier manhood, was of that exclusively agricultural character which applies itself to the cultivation of wild oats. At last he decided that he would become a painter. "

Sometime later the Dickens-Thackeray competition took an especially nasty turn. It started, apparently, when Dickens learned that Thackeray had been gossiping about Ellen Ternan. Coincidentally or not, Edmund Yates, an aspiring journalist and a Dickens family friend, published some weeks later a sneering portrait of Thackeray in a tatty London weekly. Thackeray, Yates wrote, was "cold and uninviting" as well as "openly cynical;" he was also a flatterer and a fading talent whose "success is on the wane."

Yates, Thackeray, and Dickens were all members of the Garrick Club, whose members were mainly actors, writers and patrons of the arts. Thackeray, who seems even touchier than Dickens, now demanded that the club's governing board take heed. Yates' slanderous article could not be passed off as a joke, Thackeray insisted, and Yates deserved nothing less than the club's reprimand—an official reminder that such articles were "intolerable in a society of gentlemen."

Edmund Yates

Dickens, however, took Yates' side in the ensuing squabble. His young friend, Dickens admitted, may have behaved badly, but Thackeray himself had responded intemperately by bringing the full force of his reputation against this impulsive and inexperienced person, the son of two esteemed actors, Frederick and Elizabeth Yates. The affair, which dragged on for months, brought with it legal threats and heated letters and led, finally, to Yates'

EDMUND YATES.
[Photographed by W. and A. H. Fry.]

exit from the club. Thackeray and Dickens did not speak again until 1863, not long before Thackeray's death.

In his biography of Thackeray, D. J. Taylor notes that, at the author's burial at Kensal Green, an astute American journalist gave a precise description of the very last mourner, a man "dressed not in black," but in "trousers of a check pattern, a waistcoat of some colored plaid and an open frock-coat." It was Dickens, "a look of bereavement in his face." When "all others had turned aside from the grave he still stood there, as if rooted to the spot, watching with haggardly eyes every spadeful of dust that was thrown upon it." Finally, writes Taylor, "the man began to walk away, at first with some friends, to whom he started to talk, but then finding the effort too much and dispatching them with a rapid round of handshakes so that he could leave Kensal Green alone."

William Thackeray on Charles Dickens

❝ I remember when that famous *Nicholas Nickleby* came out, seeing a letter from a pedagogue in the north of England, which, dismal as it was, was immensely comical. 'Mr Dickens's ill-advised publication,' wrote the poor schoolmaster, 'has passed like a whirlwind over the schools of the north.' He was a proprietor of a cheap school; Dotheboys' Hall was a cheap school. There were many such establishments in the northern counties. Parents were ashamed, that were never ashamed before, until the kind satirist laughed at them; relatives were frightened; scores of little scholars were taken away; poor schoolmasters had to shut their shops up; every pedagogue was voted a Squeers, and many suffered, no doubt unjustly; but afterward schoolboys' backs were not so much caned; schoolboys' meat was less tough and more plentiful; and schoolboys' milk was not so sky-blue. **❞**

LITTLE DORRIT.

1855-57

The title of Dickens' eleventh novel recalls *The Old Curiosity Shop*. Little Dorrit, however, is not entirely like Little Nell. Amy Dorrit is already a young woman; and *Little Dorrit*, like Dickens' other later novels, is mapped out with considerable care. It's less hurried, less improvisational than Dickens' first novels. It's more "realistic" too. Amy Dorrit and the novel's other key figures don't remind us of fairy tale figures. They're more like the people we know.

Still, for modern readers, Amy Dorrit might well seem as fantastic as Little Nell. She's endlessly patient and kind. She's modest and self-sacrificing— qualities perhaps less widely esteemed now than in Dickens' day. But she has also grown up in the Marshalsea—the same debtor's jail where John Dickens served time, and where neither bold confidence nor high self-esteem were much prized. Amy, moreover, is especially devoted to her father, who is both self-loathing and self-promoting, an insecure egotist with a theatrical flair. He's larger than life in his own small world. He's the self-proclaimed "Father of the Marshalsea," the head man in a colony of petty thieves.

William Dorrit is, like John Dickens, comic, pathetic, and weak. On the one hand, he is a "shabby old debtor" not much different from many of the men who come and go at the Marshalsea, where "a generation might be calculated as about three months." But Dorrit is separate from—has separated himself from—the larger population. He has lived on and on at the place for decades, setting a certain genteel tone and accepting small gratuities in return. An "unfortunate man," is how Dorrit describes himself, "but always a gentleman. Poor, no doubt, but—hum—proud. Always proud." And manipulative: William Dorrit sustains Amy's devotion by stoking her guilt. He's selfish, a bit cruel, morally shrunken. He is "Little Dorrit" too.

Finally, Dorrit is freed when a small inheritance comes his way. Suddenly, the Father of the Marshalsea is on the rise. It's a fairly common leap in Dickens' fiction: Pip, Boffin the dustman, and Mr. Chops the circus dwarf all move dramatically from the margins into the thick of High Society. Dorrit moves with his family to Italy, where the faded debtor takes his place among glittering elites. Initially, at least, the move seems fitting, for Dorrit and others in his family have warmed themselves for so long on the myth of their own superiority. Amy, though, is one of Dickens' honest souls, and free of self-flattery. She's miserable in palaces hobnobbing with the idle rich, many of whom strike her as very much like the idle poor. In a letter to Arthur Clennam, her future husband, she pleads that "you will never think of me as the daughter of a rich person; that you will never think of me as dressing any better, or living any better, than

1855-57

when you first knew me. That you will remember me only as the little shabby girl you protected with so much tenderness, from whose threadbare dress you have kept away the rain, and whose wet feet you have dried at you fire."

Of course Charles Dickens realized that not all rich people were shallow or fraudulent; that wealth, in the right hands, enriched the commonweal. Several of Dickens' closest friends, including Angela Burdett Coutts, were true philanthropists. But as a novelist Dickens repeatedly painted a darker picture of money's influence and power—of the vanity and corruption that very often comes in its wake. In *Little Dorrit* the monied monster is Mr. Merdle, whose name, suggesting *merde*, reminds us of Edward Murdstone, the wicked stepfather who torments widows and children in *David Copperfield*.

Merdle is mysterious, but much revered. He is rich, everybody knows, and has acquired an imposing wife with "an extensive bosom"—not "a bosom to repose upon," but "a capital bosom to hang jewels upon. Mr. Merdle wanted something to hang jewels upon, and he bought it for that purpose." Where Merdle goes, the magnates follow—"magnates from the Court and Magnates from the City, magnates from the Lords, magnates from the bench—all the magnates that keep us going and sometimes trip us up."

Merdle has neither obvious talents nor virtues—only this remarkable reputation for having money, taking money, and somehow making it grow. He is, Dickens laments, what passes as a great man in a materialistic age: a magnet for magnates and for toadies of every color and stripe. They bow before him as if "doing homage to some graven image." But it's a fake and hollow image: the great Merdle, his toadies discover, was "simply the greatest Forger and the greatest Thief that ever cheated the gallows."

Dickens knew the type. Greedy and fallen financiers were common enough in his day, particularly in the 1840s, when speculation in Britain's railroads grew reckless, and other Merdles, bilking investors, made out like thieves. 1847 brought a major commercial crisis triggered by bad railroad investments. George Hudson, the unscrupulous "railway king" fell in 1849, prompting much publicity. Dickens may have modeled Merdle, in part, on John Sadlier, MP, who in 1856 killed himself when his bank collapsed and his criminal dealings were disclosed.

Corruption is also symbolized in *Little Dorrit* through Dickens' satirical description of the Circumlocution Office, a fort of bureaucracy that appears to exist in order to ensure that governmental work will never get done. It is a vast, pointless place, an enclave of nepotism and arrogance, where Arthur Clennam, among others, can find neither help nor clarity. The Circumlocution Office shows the depth of Dickens disdain for politicians and their institutions—an anger that surfaces similarly in his letters. In one, sent to William Macready, Dickens says that in *Little Dorrit* he is "blowing off a little indignant steam which would otherwise blow me up." "I have lost hope even in the ballot," Dickens insists. "We appear to me to have proved the failure of representative institutions without an educated and advanced people to support them."

But *Little Dorrit* is also enriched by the presence of many vividly drawn characters, like Pancks, the scrapping rent collector who befriends the more tepid Arthur Clennam. Pancks is a shrewd if unpolished man whose hair "sticks up like a dark species of cockatoo." Pancks has been rendered machine-like in a mechanistic world: still, he's decent in his way, and vital—so "highly charged" that "one might have expected to draw sparks and snaps from him by presenting a knuckle to any part of his figure."

Pancks, moreover, shares with Amy Dorrit rare virtues that Dickens would repeatedly hail. Most of his later novels point to the pervasiveness of falseness and fakery in the world: in *Bleak House*, for example, there is the indelible image of Leicester Square on a wintry morning, where behind dingy curtains one may find a colony of conmen and "brigands" sleeping late: men with "false names, false hair, false titles, false jewelery, and false histories." Pancks, himself no stranger to the streets, has a "coaly hand." But he's earnest and sincere. There's something "indubitably genuine" in his "wonderful laugh."

Little Dorrit is a marvel of descriptive writing; here, as in *Bleak House* and *Our Mutual Friend*, the portrait of London—"so large, so barren, and so wild" as Amy Dorrit sees it—is shot-through with images both arresting and, at times, surreal. Clennam, passing at nightfall along the Strand, sees the street lamps "blessed by the foggy air, burst out one after another, like so many blazing sun-flowers coming full-blown all at once."

Some reviewers hated this dark and curious novel, and decided it offered proof of a great writer's sad decline. *Blackwood's* lamented the passing of "the old natural, easy, unconscious Pickwickian style" in favor of "something that might have come from the head of Thomas Carlyle," or "some such congenial dreary spirit."

But a more favorable review in more liberal *Leader* reminds us that while Dickens was often reproved by (mainly conservative) reviewers and publications, he was warmly embraced by others who identified with his lower middle-class origins and his progressive political views. For the *Leader*, *Little Dorrit* was something "exquisite" and rare, not least for its rendering of Merdle, who stands for "an increasing evident class of individuals not merely corrupt in themselves, but the cause of corruption in others."

Certain "university-bred reviewers," observed the *Leader*, "whose shriveled souls cannot understand the fresh, spontaneous efflorescence of genius, and will accept no gold that does not come to them impressed with the college stamp, may affect to despise the large regard of Dickens; but the world will recognize its great ones whether or not they wear the uniform of cap and gown."

CAPSULE

A TALE OF TWO CITIES.

1859

In 1859 when he was starting his research on *A Tale of Two Cities*, Dickens asked his friend Thomas Carlyle to recommend some appropriate readings. Carlyle, as if to underscore the vastness of the topic at hand, sent over a trunk loaded with books. His own book on the subject—*The French Revolution: A History*—had been both brilliantly written and deeply researched.

Apparently, Dickens didn't dip too deeply into Carlyle's large store of secondary sources. He did, however, borrow much from Caryle's book, which he had long admired and professed to have read many times. He also may have read a play, Watts Phillips' *The Dead Heart,* that had circulated in London two years before *A Tale of Cities* appeared. Phillips, apparently, thought so: both works include a heroic figure who takes another man's place at the guillotine. But then books and plays about the French Revolution had long been popular in England, and others, presumably, made use of similar figures and dramatic gestures. *The Frozen Deep*, the 1857 melodrama Dickens wrote and staged with Wilkie Collins, also features a key character rising to his highest self and dying for the woman he loves.

Whatever its sources, *A Tale of Two Cities* is easily recognized as Dickens' own. An arrogant aristocrat, the Marquis St. Evremond, is even more appalling than Lord Mulberry Hawk, caricatured in *Nicholas Nickleby.* The Marquis is smugly, brazenly indifferent to the stifling and suffering of the French people—an attitude he shares with others of his class. And this murderous indifference, Dickens' novel suggests, is precisely what brings the revolution about.

But as he had shown earlier in *Barnaby Rudge*, Dickens worried a good deal about political revolution. He had no romantic illusions about the sublimity of roused populations. His view of human nature was too dark. In *A Tale of Cities*, the Defarge family, leaders of the uprising, appear justified in the anger—and dangerous in their rage. In fact much of Dickens' political writing—and much of his charitable activity, centering on such issues as sanitation reform, and schools for workers and poor children—was inspired by his assumption that only steady, well-directed civic reforms would save Britain from its own bloody showdown. Dickens had always assumed, with varying degrees of urgency, that Britain's political leaders were in a race against time.

And he had long thought about public executions and their distinctive role in titillating base impulses and degrading public life. In 1846, in a letter published in the *Daily News*, Dickens described the bizarre and unsettling scene that surrounded him as he witnessed a fairly typical English execution. The hanging had attracted a large crowd, including many who arrived early and jostled for a better view. "No sorrow," Dickens wrote, "no salutary terror, no abhorrence, no seriousness; nothing but ribaldry, debauchery, levity, drunkenness, and flaunting vice in fifty other shapes. I should have deemed it impossible that I could have ever felt any large assemblage of my fellow-creatures to be so odious."

"I hoped, for an instant," he continued, "that there was some sense of Death and Eternity in the cry of 'Hats off!' when the miserable wretch appeared; but I found, next moment, that they only raised it as they would at a play—to see the stage better, in the final scene."

A Tale of Two Cities lent itself easily to adaptations for the stage (and much later, for the cinema) for its structure, its pace, its settings, its dialogue are highly theatrical— as if Dickens, writing the book, was simultaneously watching it, in his mind's eye, as a popular play. "Hark!" exclaims one character. "You dogs!" another. Such exclamations abound.

"I set myself the little task of making a picturesque story," Dickens told Forster, "rising in every chapter with characters true to nature, but whom the story itself should more than they should express themselves, by dialogue." As a result, *A Tale of Two Cities* is a decidedly brisk read.

What Dickens Read

....

John Forster pointed out that Dickens was often regarded with "condescending patronage or sneering irritation" by his literary contemporaries, many of whom found it annoying that such rare praise should go to a writer with so little interest in being part of Britain's intellectual class.

One of those critics, George Lewes, often appeared to enjoy putting Dickens in his place. And Forster, in his *Life of Dickens*, had fired back, dismissing Lewes' "pretentious airs" and "intolerable assumptions of an indulgent superiority."

Still, it is true that, when he was relaxing with colleagues and friends, Dickens did not generally steer the conversation toward books and ideas. He preferred to talk about the latest play he saw, as George Sala recalled, or some crime story much in the news. In later years, when he was quite free to choose his own company,

Dickens didn't seek out a circle of prominent intellectuals or university types. He favored the company of actors and cops.

But Dickens had always been an astute reader with broad-ranging tastes. His discovery, as a boy, of the great 18th-century English and Anglo-Irish writers—Smollet, Fielding, Addison, Steele, Swift—prompted him to begin seeing the world in a literary way. Dickens was also very fond of Oliver Goldsmith (1730-74), a writer of humour and sentiment, popular for such poems as "The Deserted Village" (1770) and a play, *She Stoops to Conquer* (1773), as he was for his novel, *The Vicar of Wakefield* (1766).

As a boy Dickens was also very fond of such now nearly-forgotten volumes as Mrs. Elizabeth Inchbald's *Collection of Farces* (1809) and George Coleman's *Broad Grins* (1819). Dickens often wrote of his long affection for *Robinson Crusoe* (1719) and for Defoe's other works. "Have you read the *History of the Devil?*" He asked Forster in 1837. "What a capital thing it is! I bought it for a couple of shillings yesterday and have been quite absorbed in it ever since."

Dickens' writings are not thick with classical references; after all, he knew small Latin and no Greek. But they do allude frequently, obliquely and explicitly, to the Bible, and to *The Arabian Nights*, another childhood favorite. (See for example "A Christmas Tree" and "The Thousand and One Humbugs.")

Among his contemporaries, Dickens liked much in the distinctive works of John Ruskin (1819-1900), one of the great prose writers of the age; he was drawn more ardently, however, to Thomas Carlyle (1795-1881), and joked of reading *The French Revolution* for "the 500th time." Like many prominent Victorians (including the Queen herself), Dickens also admired the essays and sermons of Sydney Smith (1771-1845), the witty and reform-minded vicar who attacked governmental corruption, backed Catholic emancipation, and helped start the

John Forster

Edinburgh Review. Dickens so loved the writings of Alfred Tennyson (1809-92) that he named his fourth son after the great Lancashire poet and laureate.

Dickens also admired Robert Browning's poems and plays, including *A Blot In the 'Scutcheon* (1843), a tragedy that, like the poet's other theatrical efforts, is not likely to see a West End revival anytime soon. For Dickens, though, *A Blot* struck home. "It has thrown me into a perfect passion of sorrow," he told Forster. It is "full of genius, natural and great thoughts, profound and yet simple and beautiful in its vigor. I know nothing in any book I have ever read, as Mildred's recurrence to that 'I was so young—I had no mother.'"

More frequently, however, Dickens alludes to Shakespeare, whose plays he had read and watched performed countless times. References to Shakespeare's plays flow with absolute ease from Dickens; they turn up continuously in his journalistic essays and, with increasing subtlety, in his novels. (But even *The Old Curiosity Shop* alludes readily to *Hamlet*, for example, as well as *Macbeth* and *Richard III*.)

From Forster's *Life*, and Dickens' letters, we learn also of the author's "respect and reverence" for the memory of Thomas Arnold, the innovative and much celebrated headmaster at Rugby; "every sentence" that Forster quoted from Arthur Stanley's *Life of Arnold* was, Dickens' wrote, "the text-book of my faith." (Some years later, the liberal-minded Stanley, the Dean of Westminster, presided over Dickens' burial and memorialization.) Dickens also praised Mrs. Gaskell's fiction, and regularly ran her ghost stories in *Household Words*. He admired the writing of Mary Ann Evans, who of course published as George Eliot, and was for some years the lover of George Lewes. After reading *Scenes of Clerical Life*, Dickens famously guessed that the author was not, in fact, a man. Dickens didn't especially care for Wordsworth's later poems or Anthony Trollope's fiction or Benjamin Disraeli's novels. (Disraeli, in turn, dubbed Dickens "Gushy.") Among his French contemporaries, Dickens particularly liked the widely popular novels of Paul de Kock.

Among Americans, Dickens favored Washington Irving's stories and William Cullen Bryant's poems. He admired Nathaniel Hawthorne, as Forster records; in fact *Mosses from an Old Manse* was "the first book he placed in my hands on his return from America, with reiterated injunctions to read it." But *The Scarlett Letter*, Dickens thought, "falls off sadly after that fine opening scene. The psychological part of the story is very much overdone, and not truly done I think." And Mr. Dimmesdale, "certainly never could have begotten" the "child out of nature," Pearl. Quite late in life, Dickens happily encountered the short fiction of Bret Harte, and found (as Forster put it) "the manner resembling himself, but the matter fresh to a degree that surprised him." Harte did revere Dickens, and—according to Mark Twain at least—tried to imitate him too closely. But Dickens found, in Harte, "the painting in all respects masterly, and the wild rude thing painted a quite wonderful reality."

Forster recalled that Dickens always journeyed or vacationed with books, including, on at least one occasion "a surprising number of books of African and other travel for which he had insatiable relish." Dickens' large library, according to his own inventory, also included, among hundreds of volumes, "Mandeville's Travels," "Holman's travels in Russia," "Prescott's Conquest of Mexico," "Fox's Martyrs" and "Voltaire's Works in French 70 vols (2 wanting)."

"*Let me recommend you, as a brother-reader of high distinction, two comedies, both Goldsmith's—She Stoops to Conquer, and The Good-natured Man. Both are so admirable and so delightfully written that they read wonderfully. A friend of mine, Forster, who wrote The Life of Goldsmith, was very ill a year or so ago, and begged me to read to him one night as he lay in bed, 'something of Goldsmith's.' I fell upon She Stoops to Conquer, and we enjoyed it with that wonderful intensity, that I believe he began to get better in the first scene, and was all right again in the fifth act.*"

—Charles Dickens to M. de Cerjat, January 1855.

Dickens On The Artist

❝ I decline to present the artist to the notice of the public as grown-up child, or as a strange, unaccountable, moon-stricken person, waiting helplessly in the street of life to be helped over the road, by the crossing-sweeper; on the contrary, I present the artist as a reasonable creature, a sensible gentleman, and as one well acquainted with the value of his time, and that of other people, as if he were in the habit of going on high 'Change every day. The Artist whom I wish to present to the notice of the Meeting is one to whom the perfect enjoyment of the five senses is essential to every achievement of his life. He can gain no wealth nor fame by buying something which he never touched, and selling it to another who would also never touch or see it, but was compelled to strike out for himself every spark of fire which lighted, burned, and perhaps consumed him. He must win the battle of life with his own hand, and with his own eyes, and was obliged to act as general, captain, ensign, non-commissioned officer, private, drummer, great arms, small arms, infantry, cavalry, all in his own unaided self. When, therefore, I ask for the artist, I do not make my appeal for one who was a cripple from his birth, but I ask it as part payment of a great debt which all sensible and civilised creatures owe to art, as a mark of respect to art, as a decoration—not as a badge—as a remembrance of what this land, or any land, would be without art, and as the token of an appreciation of the works of the most successful artists of this country. **❞**

—Charles Dickens, speaking at a dinner of the Artists' General Benevolent Institution, March 29, 1862.

Dickens on the Couch

....

The psychological analysis of Charles Dickens is there right at the start—in Forster's biography. Forster notes that his friendship with Dickens "lasted without the interruption of a day for more than three and thirty years." And Dickens, he admits, could be a puzzle, a blend of contradictions that stemmed, Forster assumed, from early years of "childish misery." Those extreme "sufferings and strugglings" spawned certain extreme reactions—a series of tendencies and preoccupations he could never quite overcome.

Forster often observed in Dickens "a too great confidence in himself, a sense that everything was possible to the will that would make it so." This showed itself in actions "hard and aggressive," in a "tone of fierceness." Something in Dickens' nature, Forster observed, "made his resolves insuperable, however hasty the opinions on which they had been formed."

And yet, right beside this "stern and even cold isolation of self reliance" was "susceptivity almost feminine" and "the most eager craving for sympathy." In *Charles Dickens* (1906), G. K. Chesterton also pointed to this "elementary antithesis" in the novelist's character," or "what appears as an antithesis in our modern popular psychology." "We are always talking about strong men against weak men," writes Chesterton, "but Dickens was not only both a weak man and a strong man, he was a very weak man and also a very strong man." He "was everything that we currently call a weak man: he was a man hung on wires; he was a man who might at any moment cry like a child; he was so sensitive to criticism that one may say that he lacked a skin."

But "in the matter where ordinary strong men are miserably weak—in the matter of concentrated toil and clear purpose and unconquerable worldly courage—he was like a straight sword." Chesterton recalled that Jane Carlyle, "who in her human epithets often hit the right nail so that it rang," once said of Dickens: "'He has a face made of steel.'" Writes Chesterton:

> This was probably felt in a flash when he she saw, in some social crowd, the clear, eager face of Dickens cutting through those near him like a knife. Any people who had met him from year to year would each year have found a man weakly troubled about his worldly decline; and each year they would have found him higher up in the world. His was a character very hard for any man of slow and placable temperament to understand; he was the character whom anybody can hurt and nobody can kill.

Glandular Organization

Dickens' life, the subject of an increasing number of sometimes sensational memoirs and biographies published during the 1920s and '30s, now drew the scrutiny of biologists and psychologists as well as literary critics and scholars. In 1936, for example, P. C. Squires, writing in the *Journal of Abnormal and Social Psychology,* declared that Dickens was of the hyperthyroid type, with well developed adrenals—the source of his "great driving power." But Dickens' parathyroids were probably subnormal, giving rise to the spasms he endured in childhood and throughout much of his life. Dickens' vanity and "foppishness," Squires reckoned, owed particularly to "an excess of post pituitary secretion." To complicate matters, Catherine Dickens, exhausted by childbearing, presented the fairly obvious case "of a somewhat myxedematous woman, giving in easily to exertion of any kind." The two, unfortunately, "were radically different in glandular organization and consequent behavior."

Edmund Wilson analyzed Dickens in his influential 1939 essay "Dickens: The Two Scrooges." As a man, Dickens was widely recognized, but little known, and largely misconstrued as a kind of literary St. Nick. But Wilson, drawing on available memoirs and biographies, as well as Dickens' own novels, showed more clearly how the tensions within Dickens revealed themselves in his work. The traumas of Dickens' childhood, Wilson wrote, prompted a hardened, if contained opposition to society that enabled him to identify creatively with outcasts and criminals—as well earnest figures seeking to do good. John Jardnyce in *Bleak House* embodies many of Dickens' sincerely felt ideals: he is kind, generous, circumspect, and capable of self-sacrifice. But Daniel Quilp, driven and cruel, also displays in an exaggerated way tendencies Dickens saw in himself. For Wilson, John Jasper in *The Mystery of Edwin Drood* well illustrates Dickens' "divided personality:" he is both "innocent and wicked," and the creation of a novelist of great "complexity and depth." Fyodor Dostoevsky, for one, saw this, but it often passed the notice of both Dickens' admirers (who seem never to have read past *A Christmas Carol*) and Dickens' debunkers who, by attacking him, were also having at all they found maudlin and sentimental in Victorian culture and art.

The Perspectives of Childhood

Wilson's essay appeared just as Freudian interpretations of literature and art were coming into vogue. Jack Lindsay's 1950 biography is frankly psychological in its approach, and makes much of Dickens' secret affair with Ellen Ternan, which had been publicized for the first time in such books as Thomas Wright's *Life of Charles Dickens* (1935) and Gladys Storey's *Dickens and Daughter* (1939). Lindsay is astute, and he esteems Dickens, but he too seems set on writing an expose—blowing apart "the Dickensian lie" in a brisk, condescending way. At least one academic reviewer of Lindsay's book lamented its "tirade" against Georgina Hogarth and its easy use of such pop-Freudian terms as "guilt-aspect" and "death wish." This critic longed for a "judicious, unbiased biography" of Charles Dickens—which Edgar Johnson, in 1952, did in fact provide.

Since then, several other thorough and judicious Dickens biographies have appeared. None are, like Lindsay's book, explicit attempts to lay bare the author's psyche. Still, all of Dickens' major biographers—including Fred Kaplan and Peter Ackroyd—have, to some degree, considered the complexity of his personality and the odd, often exasperating nature of his actions. Thus Norman and Jeanne Mackenzie, in their fine 1979 biography, surmised that Dickens had been "caught emotionally at the threshold of adolescence," and "kept transacting the unfinished business of his youth in his writings as if he might there discover some ending that had escaped him in ordinary life." The world he described, wrote the Mackenzie's, was always, to some degree, "a child's world, bewildering, full of hidden terrors, inexplicable rejection ... senseless cruelty and unexpected benevolences. Seen through a child's eye, life is so episodic, so full of rich detail,

"He was the character that anybody can hurt and nobody can kill."

—G.K. Chesterton

so brimming with energy." But, "the problems of adult life cannot be properly stated let alone understood and solved, even by the cleverest child. And even the cleverest adult cannot cope with them, maturely, when his vision of the world is shaped by the perspectives of childhood and colored by its enduring resentments"—something Dickens himself recognized, as his 1848 Christmas book *The Haunted Man* shows.

At least one critic, the Scottish writer David Craig, resented the way "blasé critics" tried to "cut Dickens down to size" by suggesting, explicitly or not, that he exaggerated his "childhood traumas" and was, in any event, "not alone" in either enduring, or describing the multitude of evils that a poor child in the 1820s could face. Dickens, wrote Craig, was "(a) neither an ordinary reforming publicist nor a neurotic at the mercy of his own compulsions: he was a man with a character so powerful and creative that whatever happened to him both bit deep and, later, fired him to create remarkable images of experiences which he was not alone in having" and "(b) his intensely observant and responsive nature, further sharpened by years of journalism, fitted him to be a particularly good, and not a particularly eccentric or distorting, witness to social facts from which his novels started."

But on this subject perhaps Dickens himself should be allowed the last word. In his 1853 essay, "Gone Astray," Dickens writes: "They used to say I was an odd child, and I suppose I was. I am an odd man perhaps."

Dickens
on Film

....

Film versions of Dickens' novels and stories are as old as commercial cinema it- self. In the late 1890s, quite a few American, British, and French filmmakers went to *Oliver Twist* and *A Christ- mas Carol* for material; in the early 1900s, silent versions of *The Old Curiosity Shop* and "Dolly Varden" (based on *Barnaby Rudge*) also appeared. In 1909 D.W. Griffith, who claimed Dickens as an influence, offered his version of *The Cricket on the Hearth*—six years before his epic, *The Birth of a Nation*, made him famous, and infamous.

Other early adaptations include the Vitagraph studio's 1911 version of *A Tale of Two Cities*, significant for its relatively big bud- get and length; this tale was released on three reels—a significant advance at the time. In 1917, a five-reel version of *Great Expecta- tions* appeared, joined by an even longer British version of *Little Dorrit*. As their technology improved, filmmakers were more will- ing to tackle, however imperfectly, Dickens' more ambitious nov- els. A 1922 version of *Oliver Twist* starred Lon Chaney as Fagin and, as Oliver, Jackie Coogan, the era's leading child star.

Hollywood discovered Dickens in a bigger way during the

1930s, the first full decade of sound. At MGM David Selznick produced *David Copperfield* (1935) and *A Tale of Two Cities* (1935), an especially lavish and, in its way, thoughtful production that starred Ronald Colman and a cast of thousands. Universal Studios released *Great Expectations* (1934) and *The Mystery of Edwin Drood* (1935)—not a surprising choice for the studio that also made *Dracula* (1931) and *Frankenstein* (1931) in much the same spooky, melodramatic manner.

During the 1940s and 1950s, the best Dickens films were, not surprisingly, British, led by David Lean's much celebrated *Great Expectations* (1946) and his *Oliver Twist* (1948), a film noir masterpiece that features Alec Guinness in a performance as Fagin that grasps exactly what Dickens was after; that is both stagy and subtle and, on film at least, has never been surpassed. The Ealing Studios' *Nicholas Nickleby* (1947) still holds up well: its distinguished cast includes Cedric Hardwicke, Sybil Thorndike, and Stanley Holloway.

1951 saw the release of *Scrooge*, a rather loose adaptation of *A Christmas Carol* starring the gifted farceur Alastair Sim as Scrooge and, as Marley, Michael Hordern, whose sudden appearance as a screaming ghost draped in chains still sends chills. In 1952 Noel Langley, who scripted *Scrooge*, directed *The Pickwick*

Colin Hurley as David Copperfield

Papers, with James Hayter in the title role. "James Hayter *Is* Pickwick!" This time, such hype would be true. Rarely has a film actor so convincingly embodied a famous literary character. Hayter heads a delightful cast in a film that has remained quite fresh over the years.

Carol Reed's *Oliver!* (1968) is, of course, one of the most successful film musicals ever, and features Oliver Reed as an especially menacing Bill Sikes. Ron Moody, who plays Fagin here, returns as Uriah Heep in Delbert Mann's *David Copperfield* (1969), a rather too tightly condensed, big-budget television version that does include

Ralph Richardson's nice turn as Micawber and Malcolm Arnold's fine musical score. *Oliver!* sparked other Dickens-derived musical projects for television and film, including *Pickwick* (1969) with Harry Secombe; *Scrooge* (1970) with Albert Finney; *Smike!* (1973) with Ian Sharrock; and *Mr. Quilp* (1975), with Anthony Newley. Producers also envisioned *Pip!*—a musical version of *Great Expectations* starring Michael York. But the score was dropped, and *Pip!* became simply *Great Expectations* (1974) with York neatly playing Pip, Anthony Quayle taking on Jaggers, and with James Mason lending, to Magwitch, a certain gruff gravity that becomes the self-proclaimed grubber quite well.

Throughout the 1970s, the BBC offered a series of well-acted, well-scripted Dickens productions, including a 1974 version of *David Copperfield* that retains its low-budget charm and boasts distinctive performances by comedic veterans Arthur Lowe as Wilkins Micawber, and Patricia Routledge as Micawber's wife.

In 1976, Yorkshire TV produced *Dickens of London*, a ten-part dramatization of Dickens' life based on Wolf Mankowitz's insightful and affectionate script; Roy Dotrice is splendid as Charles and John Dickens, and Gene Foad, as the younger Dickens, offers an entirely convincing picture of Boz in the first blaze of success.

Ronald Colman in A Tale of Two Cities

Granada TV's *Hard Times* (1977), directed by John Irvin, is also striking: its opening sequence, showing Sleary's circus entrance into Coketown (Manchester, actually) is particularly well-done—a superb capturing of both the novel's mood and Dickens' larger literary intent.

The 1980s now look like a golden age of Dickens film and television adaptations; clearly, the controversy and tumult that came in the wake of Margaret Thatcher's conservative revolution also sparked a renewed interest in the novelist most widely associated with themes of wealth and poverty. The lengthy

1982 television adaptation of *Nicholas Nickleby*, based on the Royal Shakespeare Company's stage production, led the way. No less ambitious was Christine Edzard's *Little Dorrit*, a 1988 feature film that is very long, highly original, and yet true to its source. Alec Guinness' William Dorrit is a marvel here, and brought the actor his fifth Academy Award nomination.

The BBC offered, in 1983, a very good *Dombey and Son*, with Julian Glover in the title role, and—in 1985—a spirited version of *The Pickwick Papers*. In the same year the BBC also aired adaptations of *Oliver Twist* and *Bleak House*—a widely acclaimed version starring Peter Vaughan (Tulkinghorn) and Diana Rigg (Lady Dedlock). Two more notable televison adaptations appeared during the decade: the BBC's *David Copperfield* (1986) and *A Tale of Two Cities* (1989), a first-rate collaboration between Granada TV and Dune Studios, France.

Many of the later video adaptations of Dickens' books have, in fact, been collaborations—most notably between the BBC and the American Public Broadcasting System. But meanwhile the Disney Company offered two very good Dickens productions, including *Great Expectations* (1989), with John Rhys-Davies as a particularly strong Joe Gargery, and *The Old Curiosity Shop* (1995), in which Tom Courtenay, who fortunately for him looks nothing like Daniel Quilp, effectively conveys the monstrous villain's demonic zeal.

Some of the most popular Dickens television versions have appeared since the mid-1990s, as higher production values have combined, in some cases, with inspired casting and notable scripts. In 1994, the BBC released, in multiple episodes, *Martin Chuzzlewit*, a thoroughly successful production which benefits from David Lodge's smart adaptation and by exceptional performances by Paul Scoffield as Old Martin and Tom Wilkinson as Pecksniff. The BBC's latest *Bleak House* (2005), shown in fifteen weekly episodes, also helped make Dickens a bestselling author once more. Some critics objected that the production, and Andrew Davies' script, strayed a bit too far from its original source; more, however, hailed its inventiveness and verve, and its stimulating way of making one of Dickens' darker novels vivid in the video age. The strong cast includes Denis Lawson (John Jardnyce), Anna Maxwell Martin (Esther Summerson), Nathaniel Parker (Horace Skimpole), Charles Dance (Tulkinghorn) and Burn Gorman as the definitive William Guppy.

CAPSULE

GREAT EXPECTATIONS.

1860-61

Close readers of Dickens will recognize the consistency of his themes and the regularity of his fictional types. In Dickens' world one finds naïve young men on a collision course with reality. There are older men with cramped views and few interests beyond money and work. There are various characters wallowing in self-pity as life goes by. There are gentle or passive figures crushed by fate or, more happily, accorded some haven in the battle of life. There are dominators, compulsives, monomaniacs: a well-stocked gallery of the selfish and the self-absorbed.

In Dickens' fiction, selfishness and pride are frequent targets of satirical scorn. But his books are also informed by a strong sense of right and wrong—by an endorsement of moral decency presented straightforwardly, and without irony. In *Great Expectations* Joe Gargery's life exemplifies, in its small sphere, decency, generosity, forgiveness. Joe, like many of Dickens' most admirable characters, thinks of others and not only of himself. In certain ways, Joe's calm and benevolent spirit infuses this novel, which is more leanly structured and subdued than previous works.

Pip, the narrator, is the naive young man here—another of Dickens' poor orphans. Pip lives with his older sister, a bony, red-faced woman who beats the boy and calls him "a young monkey" among other things. Obviously Pip's sister resents the task of raising her much younger brother, just as she resents everything else; she never smiles or laughs but instead lets loose great torrents of abuse directed at Pip and her blacksmith husband, the long suffering Joe. She does have a certain circle of friends—a grim lot of self-important eccentrics who, Pip notes, actively hate him too.

Joe is strong, quiet, and illiterate: he works hard at his forge, but he projects a certain thoughtful air. At first, Joe's a bit of a puzzle for both Pip and the reader—what sort of man would stay married to an abusive woman who wears a coarse apron that "was stuck full of pins" as if in "a strong reproach against Joe." He is masochistic, one thinks, and deluded. Pip describes his brother-in-law as "mild, good-natured, sweet-tempered, easygoing, foolish."

But Joe, although unschooled, is sensitive, and no less effected by his rough childhood than Esther Summerson was by hers. Joe's father was often drunk and "hammered" his wife and family. Joe then is accustomed to abuse, but certain too that his flawed father had some good in his "hart." Joe, who looks for the good in people, is also certain that Pip's sister—"a fine figure of a woman"—has qualities of her own, deep down. Apparently he senses within her some sorry restlessness which he also understands. In any event, as he tells Pip: "I see so much in my poor mother of a woman drudging and slaving and breaking her honest hart and never getting no peace in her mortal days, that I'm dead afeerd of going wrong in the way of not doing what's right by a woman, and I'd fur rather of the two go wrong the t'other way, and be a little ill-conwenienced myself."

"Never," Aunt Betsey tells David Copperfield, "be mean in anything: never be false; never be cruel. Avoid these three vices, Trot, and I can always be hopeful of you." Poor Joe is socially awkward and he's afraid of his wife. But he is also an exemplar of Betsey Trotwood's three principles. Pip calls him "a sort of Hercules in strength, and also in weakness."

Dickens' novels are, then, for all of their complexity, allegories of a sort: over and over again characters exhibit obvious failings—vices—that undo them in the end. Miss Havisham, like Aunt Betsey, long ago suffered the blow of a broken romance and was left, in her wedding dress, to consider the perfidy found in the hearts of men. But unlike David's aunt, she went no further, allowing "wild resentment" and "wounded pride" to shadow her days. She trains Estella, the young girl in her care, to share in her misery. Estella—as Pip's friend Herbert Pocket puts it—is "hard and haughty to the last degree, and has been brought up to wreak revenge on all the male sex."

Our early environments shape us indelibly: it's another common theme in Dickens' work. Pip, belittled by his sister, learned to say little and expect less. When he finds himself taken up by Miss Havisham, he reverts instantly to his passive role. He cannot see that Miss Havisham is a lunatic, or that Estella is herself damaged, her soul turned to ice. Pip utterly accepts Estella's "air of completeness and superiority." And he walks with "submission" at her side.

Of course Pip projects a more confident side when, to his complete surprise, he finds himself rich. He doesn't question his hope that the mysterious Miss Havisham is his anonymous patron, and—in his attempt to please her and win Estella as well—he sets forth to rise in the world and leave Joe's forge far behind. He moves to London, buys new clothes, joins a circle of smart fellows, and lives large. Pip is too naïve and ignorant to do much else with his new fortune, and too obsessed with Estella to add up his debts or the consequences of his actions. Pip is a fraud, and he becomes a gentleman without means—a type Dickens knew well. Pip in his extravagant posturing not only wounds Joe, but he corrupts his roommate, Pocket. "My lavish habits," he admits, led Pocket's "easy nature into expenses he could not afford, corrupted the simplicity of his life, and disturbed his peace with anxieties and regrets." Corrupt and disturb; breed anxiety, regret: this, in Dickens' world, is what money tends to do.

John Dickens, perhaps, haunts *Great Expectations* just as he haunts

David Copperfield and *Little Dorrit*. In this novel, he might be represented by Abel Magwitch, the gruff ex-con who, after disappearing into Australia, returns to England and identifies himself as Pip's silent benefactor. He has repaid Pip's kindness of years before by ensuring that the young man becomes a "gentleman"—one of those words, like "respectable," that in Dickens is often loaded with irony. Magwitch has neither the pedigree nor the mien to reach such a lofty station himself, so he has done it vicariously. And Pip, no matter what lofty social station he reaches, will know always that he owes it all to the convict he first glimpsed, in a graveyard, fleeing the law and dragging his chains.

"Look'ee here, Pip," Magwitch tells him, "I'm your second father. You're my son—more to me nor any son." John Dickens, one assumes, was not this crude: surely he wasn't in the habit of eating in an "uncouth, noisy, and greedy" way before announcing "I'm a heavy grubber." Still, John Dickens was long a source of embarrassment to his son. He was, in his younger years, a rather vulgar social climber with great expectations of his own: the son of servants who briefly kept servants of his own. But he was also a criminal, so diffuse and delinquent in his indebtedness that he spent time in jail. Charles' success was much harder to get, and far more enduring. But there was John Dickens, still shabby and cadging funds until the end of his days—the tragicomic symbol of the past his son could never quite shake.

EATING AS A FINE ART.

(*From the " New York Daily Graphic."*)

Dickens and Macready

....

Charles Dickens was not an introvert; he enjoyed the company of a wide circle of colorful and interesting acquaintances and friends. From the start Dickens' social circle included many literary and theatrical figures, including William Charles Macready, one of the best-known English actors of the day. Macready was an intense, introspective perfectionist, like Dickens himself. He was similarly sensitive to criticism, fond of France, and found what he called "meditative tranquility" hard to find. ("*My greatest enemy*," Macready once wrote, "*the stumbling block of my life*, has been *passion*, and its consequent evil, precipitation.") And like Dickens Macready had a rather difficult relationship with his own father, a theatre manager who, after some success, went broke.

Unlike Dickens, Macready left behind a frank and lengthy diary that offers revealing glimpses of many of the key figures in the Dickens circle. Thus Macready records his frequent exasperation with John Forster, a longtime advisor and friend. In 1838 Macready criticizes Forster for "goading" the overworked Dickens into writing a farce that, in Macready's view, was not up the young writer's standard. Forster, writes Macready, is the "most indiscreet friend that ever allied himself to any person." Forster often "embroils his friends in difficulties and distresses in this most officious manner. It is quite bad."

Macready was already an accomplished actor and theater director (of both Covent Garden and Drury Lane) when, in 1842, he agreed to mind Dickens' young children while Boz and his wife Catherine sailed off for their long, ill-fated trip to the United States. Macready had visited the States in the 1820s, and he shared Dickens' sense of what was admirable—and detestable— in the new nation. Certainly the letters Dickens sent Macready from America are especially dramatic, full of stark fulminations. "I believe," thundered Dickens in one letter, "the heaviest blow ever dealt at Liberty's head will be dealt by this nation in the ultimate failure of its example to the earth. See what is passing now! Look at the exhausted treasury. The paralyzed Government, the unworthy representatives of a free people, the desperate contests between the North and the South…the stabbing and shootings and coarse and brutal threatening exchanged between Senators under the very Senate's roof—the intrusion of the most pitiful, mean, malicious, creeping, crawling, sneaking party spirit into all transactions of life—even into the appointments of physicians to pauper madhouses—the silly driveling, slanderous, wicked, monstrous Party Press."

Dickens' complaints proved particularly prophetic when, in 1848, Macready returned to the States and his widely-publicized rivalry with the American actor Edwin Forrest turned unexpectedly violent. A group of Forrest's more ardent fans sparked a riot during Macready's performance at New York's Astor Place Opera House. More than a dozen people were killed in the melee, and Macready barely escaped without harm. "I feel I cannot stomach the United States as a nation," Macready wrote in 1846. "The good there, I must admit, appears like the quantity of the grains of wheat to the bushel of chaff."

Like Dickens, Macready came to devote considerable energy to charitable causes, particularly to the education of the poor. The two shared similar political views. They were keenly critical of public policy in Britain, where the bleak effects of urban poverty were everywhere to be seen. "I do not think there is justice in this country," Macready wrote in 1842, using words that would recall Dickens own. "I am really sickened with the utter absence of truth throughout the social system that tyranny and priestcraft have built up. … I wonder that the downtrodden mass does not rise up. It is a world of suffering; but why we should have no choice in being a part of it is what I cannot comprehend. My state of mind is one of *agony*." Dickens, of course, would often mock in his novels the tendency to morbidness and self-pity that Macready's diaries often display. Still, the two men—actors both—were very much alike in many ways.

THE CHARACTERS OF CHARLES DICKENS

POURTRAYED IN A SERIES OF ORIGINAL WATER COLOUR SKETCHES BY KYD

THE CHARACTERS OF CHARLES DICKENS ARE SOMETHING MORE THAN MERE FICTIONAL CREATIONS, MERE CREATURES OF THE IMAGINATION; THEY BREATHE AND LIVE IN REAL FLESH AND BLOOD, THEY EXIST IN OUR VERY MIDST. WE KNOW OR SEEM TO HAVE KNOWN THEM PERSONALLY; WE HAVE SMILED WITH SAM WELLER, WE HAVE SYMPATHIZED WITH TINY TIM, WE HAVE WEPT WITH LITTLE NELL. THEY WILL CEASE TO CHARM US ONLY WHEN THE ENGLISH LANGUAGE IS FORGOTTEN, OR HUMAN NATURE CEASES TO EXIST.

RAPHAEL TUCK & SONS, LONDON, PARIS & NEW YORK.
Printed at the Fine Art Works in London.

OUR MUTUAL FRIEND.

1864-65

This is Dickens' final completed novel. In many ways, it shows how far Dickens had traveled from those early days when, as Graham Greene once put it, he had "hit on a mine" with *Oliver Twist* and other early novels that had "paid him a tremendous dividend. Fielding and Smollett, tidied and refined for the new industrial bourgeoisie, had both salted it; Goldsmith had contributed sentimentality and Monk Lewis horror."

Our Mutual Friend also has its share of odd and fantastical elements, as well as touches of sentimentality and whimsy. It finds its way, finally, to a happy ending. And London certainly looms large in *Our Mutual Friend*—just it does in *Oliver Twist*. But *Our Mutual Friend* is constructed by a much more sophisticated writer, one in full control of his own voice and with a firm sense of literary design.

The author of *Our Mutual Friend* has found his theme, and has certainly learned to play it in a variety of elaborate ways. That theme, as one of the novel's characters puts it, is "money, money, and what money can make of life." In *Our Mutual Friend* that theme is played in a very dark key.

The book is long, and over the years its tone has put some readers off. Henry James was one. In 1865 the young novelist took his own poke at the English-speaking world's most popular novelist. James does not, fortunately, compare Dickens unfavourably to Thackeray. But he's convinced that Dickens is artistically worn out and essentially serving up his usual mix of "very cheap merriment and very cheap pathos." *Our Mutual Friend*, writes James, is "the poorest of Mr. Dickens' works." It "is wanting in inspiration." For at least a decade, James suggests, Dickens "has been unmistakenly forcing himself. *Bleak House* was forced; *Little Dorrit* was laboured; the present work is dug out as with a spade and pickaxe." "Seldom," writes James, have "we read a book so intensely written, so little seen, known, or felt."

But many years later, other critics were willing to look more sympathetically at this long and distinctive novel, and its reputation continues to rise. In 1950, for example, Dickens biographer Jack Lindsay gave *Our Mutual Friend* his unqualified praise. For Lindsay, this is "one of the greatest works of prose ever written, a work which finally vindicates Dickens' right to stand, as no other English writer can stand, at the side of Shakespeare."

The novel's plot is "extraordinarily complex," as John Sutherland writes, "verging on impenetrability." It revolves, like *Bleak House*, around a will—and the large fortune John Harmon left his son. Harmon built his fortune on "dust," or waste in all of its forms: the detritus of urban industrial life. Harmon, a Dust Contractor, hauled it, piled it, sold it, recycled it. He built an

1864-65

estate "with its own mountain range, like an old volcano," formed by "Dust. Coal-dust, vegetable-dust, bone-dust, crockery-dust, rough-dust, and sifted-dust—all manner of Dust."

But the younger John Harmon gains his father's wealth only if he marries Bella Wilfer—someone he doesn't know. John, however, is reported dead, and so it appears that the vast pile derived from the vast piles of waste will pass permanently to Nicodemus Boffin, the Dust Tycoon's most trusted employee. In fact Boffin and his wife, neither of them sophisticates, now begin to appear as people of means. They befriend Bella Wilfer, the daughter of a clerk, who is described by her mother as an "incarnation of sauciness."

Bella is pretty, petulant, and determined to marry a wealthy man. "I am," she proclaims with a certain humorous sense of self-dramatization, "the most mercenary little wretch that ever lived in the world." "It's not that I care for money to keep as money, but I do care so much for what it will buy!" "I am," she admits, "always avariciously scheming."

John Harmon, it turns out, isn't dead; instead, under the name of John Rokesmith, he takes lodgings with Bella's family in order to observe more closely his designated fiancé.

Meanwhile, another plot flows through *Our Mutual Friend*. It centers around Lizzie Hexam, the daughter of another, less-accomplished dustman of sorts. Gaffer Hexam trolls the Thames by night in the hope of fishing out bits of money and other valuables, even if he finds them in the pockets of the freshly drowned. "What world does a dead man belong to?" he reasons. "T'other world. What world does money belong to? This world."

Lizzie's suitors include a schoolteacher, Bradley Headstone, one of a long series of young men in Dickens' fiction struggling to overcome rough circumstances and rise. Bradley dresses up in a "decent black coat and waistcoat, and decent white shirt, and decent formal black tie." He appears to be "a throroughly decent young man of six-and-twenty." Still, he looks awkward in such a costume, "recalling some mechanics in their holiday clothes." There was "a kind of settled trouble in the face. It was the face belonging to a naturally slow or inattentive intellect that had toiled hard to get what it had won, and that had to hold it now that it was gotten. He always seemed to be uneasy lest anything should be missing from his mental warehouse, and taking stock to assure himself."

In the end Dickens links it all together, more or less, introducing some of his most memorable characters along the way. There is Hamilton Veneering, who is all surface, as his name implies. Veneering, self-made and self-satisfied, is another vulgar aspirant to the tacky pleasures of High Society; he takes a seat in Parliament despite a complete lack of well-informed political views. There is Mr. Venus, one of Dickens' most vivid secondary characters—a sketchy, moody, tea-swilling taxidermist who keeps a shop filled with bones and skins and various preserved artifacts and who, to his great regret, loves a woman who looks down on his trade.

1864-65

Our Mutual Friend is, in fact, filled with dodgy characters—schemers, fortunehunters, and moneylenders like "Fascination" Fledgeby, who is fascinated by little beyond the prospect of ready financial gain. Fledgeby exploits Aaron Riah, an employee, "an old Jewish man in an ancient coat"—a "venerable" figure whose decent impulses stand out in this murky world of shameless self-seeking.

Jenny Wren is another good soul, and quite strong in her way—one of countless Londoners who, Dickens suggests, carry on with admirable pluck in the battle of life. Jenny has a certain talent, and a capacity for imaginative self-invention. She parents her drunkard father, a "tottering wretch" convincingly portrayed. She runs a small business making dresses for dolls. "Very difficult to fit too," Jenny notes, "because their figures are so uncertain. You never know where to expect their waists."

There is also Betty Higden, whom Dickens similarly salutes. Betty is one of those women "who by dint of an indomitable purpose and a strong constitution fight out many years, though each year has come with its new knock-down blows fresh to fight against her." She is "an active old woman, with a bright dark eye and a resolute face, yet quite a tender creature too; not a logically-reasoning woman, but God is good, and hearts may count in Heaven as high as heads."

Betty tends children for four pence a week. She gets by, but fears above all else the indignity of dying in the poor house. For like *Oliver Twist* this novel also makes clear Dickens' belief that Great Britain, for all of its power and wealth, had yet to find humane ways of tending to the basic needs of the deserving poor.

Betty knows how "the worn-out people," fate's unfortunates, "get driven from post to pillar and pillar to post, a-purpose to tire them out! Do I ever read how they are put off, put off, put off how they are grudged, grudged, grudged, the shelter, or the doctor, or the drop of physic, or the bit of bread? Do I never read how they grow heartsick of it and give it up, after having let themselves drop so low, and how they all die out for want of help? Then I say, I hope I can die as well as another, and I'll die without that disgrace."

Betty, though, does know the kindness of others; there is the young man Sloppy, another oddly colorful struggler, who—as Betty explains—"took his name from being found on a Sloppy night." Sloppy is amiable and sympathetic, and he amuses Betty Higden by reading to her from the newspaper. "And I do love a newspaper," she declares. "You mightn't think it, but Sloppy is a beautiful reader of the newspaper. He do the Police in different voices."

And there is John Podsnap, who appears early on in the novel as a symbol of much that Dickens found appalling in British society. Podsnap is, in fact, a recognizable target for readers of Dickens' fiction and journalism—a pompous, blustering man of means who denies the existence of the poor, and happily assumes that those who can't cope with life must necessarily be swept away. Dickens calls this attitude "Podsnappery"—and its roots are clearly in the Ebenezer Scrooge School of Economics and Public Policy.

At the start of his career, Dickens had often implied that he was "pillorying abstract faults in the manner of the comedy of humors," as Edmund Wilson put it, targeting selfishness in *Martin Chuzzlewit* and, pride in *Dombey and Son*. "But the truth," writes Wilson in "Dickens: The Two Scrooges," was "that he had already begun an indictment against a specific society: the self-important and moralizing middle class who had been making such rapid progress in England and coming down like a damper on the bright fires of English life—that is, on the spontaneity and gaiety, the frankness and independence, the instinctive human virtues, which Dickens admired and trusted."

Podsnap owes something to the blustering John Forster; it was long Dickens' habit to borrow, for his characters, certain traits and marked idiosyncracies from his acquaintances and friends. (In *Bleak House*, the writer Leigh Hunt inspired Horace Skimpole, and the poet Walter Savage Landor was, apparently, a model for the more attractively robust Laurence Boythorn. Dickens borrowed from family members as well, and Bella very probably owes something of her wilfulness and fiery nature to Dickens' eldest daughter Kate.)

Still, it's also possible to see Podsnap as a more finished portrait of Alderman Cute, one of the windy boors who bullies Trotty Veck in *The Chimes*. Like Cute, Podsnap readily dismisses all unpleasantries that don't accord squarely with his settled view of the world. "I don't choose to discuss it," Podsnap asserts. "I don't admit it." Podsnap "had even acquired a peculiar flourish of his right arm in often clearing the world of its most difficult problems, by sweeping them behind him (and consequently sheer away) with those words and a flushed face. For they affronted him."

Podsnap conducts business "with other countries," but on the whole he considers other countries "a mistake," dismissing all manners and customs that are not verifiably English. In a particularly hilarious scene, Dickens describes Podsnap at a dinner party haranguing a French guest whose English is poor. Podsnap demands: "'How Do You Like London?'" as if he were "administering something in the nature of a powder or potion to a deaf child." "'London, Londres, London?' You find it Very Large? And very Rich?' The foreign gentleman found it, without doubt, enormement riche."

"'Enormously Rich, We say,' returned Mr. Podsnap, in a condescending manner. 'Our English adverbs do Not terminate in Mong and we pronounce the "ch" as if there were a "t" before it. We Say Ritch.'

'Reetch,' remarked the foreign gentleman.'

'And Do You Find, Sir,' pursued Mr. Podsnap, with dignity, 'Many Evidences that Strike You, of our British Constitution in the Streets Of The World's Metropolis, London, Londres, London?'

The foreign gentleman begged to be pardoned, but did not altogether understand.

'The Constitution Britannique,' Mr. Podsnap explained, as if he were teaching in an infant school. 'We Say British,

But You Say Britannique, You Know (forgivingly, as if it were not his fault.)" 'The Constitution, Sir.'

The foreign gentleman said, 'Mais, yees; I know eem. ...

'I was Inquiring,' said Mr. Podsnap, resuming the thread of his discourse, 'Whether You Have Observed in our Streets as We should say, Upon our Pavvy as You would say, any Tokens—'

The foreign gentleman with patient courtesy entreated pardon; 'But what was tokenz?'

'Marks,' said Mr. Podsnap; 'Signs, you know, Appearances—Traces.'

'Ah! Of a Orse?' inquired the foreign gentleman.

'We call it Horse,' said Mr. Podsnap, with forbearance. 'In England, Angleterre, England, We Aspirate the "H," and we say "Horse," Only our Lower Classes Say "Orse!"

Pardon,' said the foreign gentleman; 'I am alwiz wrong!"'

When another guest, a man of "meek demeanor" notes that "some half-dozen people had lately died in the streets of starvation," Podsnap's response is blunt: "'I don't believe it.'" The meek guests points to "the Inquests and the Registrar's returns." Again, Podsnap is without doubt: "'Then it was their own fault,'" for "'there is not a country in the world, sir, where so noble a provision is made for the poor as in this country.'" The meek man suggests, then, that inquiries should be made; if something went wrong, somewhere, permitting such a rare event to occur, "'wouldn't it be well to try, very seriously, to find out where?'"

"'Ah!' said Mr. Podsnap. 'Easy to say somewhere; not so easy to say where! But I see what you are driving at. I knew it from the first. Centralization. No. Never with my consent. Not English.'"

England, in Dickens' fictional world, gets less and less green. *Bleak House* had surveyed London and found little to rest the soul or please the eye. Fog fills the streets; "smoke," that novel tells us, "is the London ivy." And everywhere there is "the street mud, which is made of nobody knows what, and collects about us nobody knows whence or how: we only knowing in general that when there is too much of it, we find it necessary to shovel it away."

Our Mutual Friend describes London in much the same way. It's a gloomy city, full of shysters, scavengers, and soot. In the evening especially "London city has not a hopeful aspect. The closed warehouses and offices have an air of death about them, and the national dread of colour has an air of mourning. The towers and steeples of the many house-encompassed churches, dark and dingy as the sky that seems descending on them, are no relief to the general gloom; a sundial on a church-wall has the look, in its useful black shade, of having failed in its business enterprise and stopped payment for ever; melancholy waifs and strays of housekeepers and porters sweep melancholy waifs and strays of papers and pins into the kennels, and other more melancholy waifs and strays explore them, searching and stooping and poking for anything to sell. The set of humanity toward the City is as a set of prisoners departing from gaol, and dismal Newgate [a prison] seems quite as fit a stronghold for the mighty Lord

1864-65

Mayor as his own state-dwelling."

At first, sales of *Our Mutual Friend* were strong—helped by a heavy advertising campaign. Dickens' publishers, Chapman and Hall, spent over a thousand pounds promoting the novel through handbills and posters. But sales sank steadily; by the time the final installment appeared, sales had dropped by half. *The Saturday Review,* like Henry James, called it a "very tedious performance."

Edmund Wilson, writing in the late 1930s, was among the first to note the novel's complexity and art; its elaborate underscoring of many of the writer's most persistent themes; and its departure from certain formulas that Dickens had used frequently in the past. He notes, for example, that just as the middle class "has become a monster" in *Our Mutual Friend*, so "the gentry have taken on an aspect more attractive than we have ever known them to wear as a class in any previous novel of Dickens." In earlier Dickens novels, the "frivolous and idle young man of good family"— say, James Harthouse in *Hard Times* or Henry Gowan in *Little Dorrit* was always exhibited as "more or less of a scoundrel."

But here, at least, several largely sympathetic figures—including the Reverend Frank Milvey, Mortimer Lightwood, and Eugene Wrayburn, Lizzie Hexam's husband-to-be—are all "remnants of an impoverished gentry." Otherwise, as Wilson writes, you find "the decent values" in *Our Mutual Friend* among "an impoverished proletariat and lower middle class: the modest clerk, the old Jew, the dolls' dressmaker, the dust con-

tractor's foreman, the old woman who minds children for a living"—in other words, where you always "decent values" in Dickens' fiction.

Our Mutual Friend, as Wilson notes, conspicuously brings these two classes together when Lizzie—the "illiterate daughter of a Thames-side water-rat"— becomes Wrayburn's wife. Writes Wilson: "Dickens has here, for the first time in his novels, taken his leading woman from the lowest class; and it will the principal moral of *Our Mutual Friend* that Wrayburn will have the courage to marry Lizzie." Moreover, "the inevitable conjunction of the high with the low is not here to result in a tragedy but to figure as a fortunate affair."

In fact, "the final implication" of *Our Mutual Friend*, writes Wilson, "is—to state it in the Marxist language—that the declassed representatives of the old professional upper classes may unite with the proletariat against the commercial middle class." It's a point that Peter Ackroyd makes similarly in his expansive 1990 Dickens biography. In middle life, for Dickens, it is "the need for co-operation between the classes that lies at the heart of his design, and indeed is the one theme to which he reverts again and again in his public speeches, amounting to a demand for '...a fusion of several classes on a good, common, mutual ground.'"

"That is why," Ackroyd continues, "despite his private distaste for the 'aristocratic' class, in public at least he continually urged the connection of class with class for the purposes of mutual benefit. 'I wish to avoid placing in opposition here,' he had said during his

1864-65

speech to the Administrative Reform Association, 'the two words Aristocracy and People. I am one of those who can belive in the virtues and uses of both, and, I would elevate or depress neither, at the cost of a single just right belonging to either.'" Dickens, rightly associated with many liberal reforms, was then, as Ackroyd notes, "often expressly conservative in his real social attitudes."

More recently, the English novelist Melvin Bragg also found himself newly impressed by *Our Mutual Friend,* and with the "powerful sense of goodness" with which Dickens could endow a character. Thus Sloppy: shambling, sensitive, and loyal. "Who, I wonder," writes Bragg, "is writing about Sloppy today; who would think him worthwhile? He is not only part of an underclass, he is an unglamorous, unexciting part of an underclass, and yet Dickens shows us that his virtue is a prop to society and a shining characteristic in itself. As with Betty Higden and others, Dickens draws us in so we believe, against great odds, that there is a good world somewhere whose location is not in any one class or set of circumstances but spread all around the place in the unlikeliest hovel and in the most light-feathered head."

"It is not a very modern experience," Bragg continues, "to spend time in a book being steered towards the better while full account is taken of the worst. And yes, sometimes Dickens does fancify too glibly as when he describes the mill workers coming out on a Saturday night and somehow being part of the scene of pastoral serendipity."

But, writes Bragg, "he can be allowed to nod. Inside *Our Mutual Friend,* besides the plot, the stories, the Podsnaps, Mr. Venus and Silas Wegg… inside that great caravan of fiction is a scroll being taken across the sands, a scroll proclaiming that only by doing good will the world be fit to live in."

"It would be a bold author who would argue as much explicitly and with all his genius today. And an even bolder author who would dare produce so many happy endings."

CAPSULE

THE MYSTERY OF EDWIN DROOD.

1870

Dickens wrote much of this unfinished novel at Gad's Hill, his country home near Rochester, Kent. Dickens had spent the happiest years of his childhood in this area, and it's fitting that his last work of fiction should draw closely on the atmosphere of Rochester, an old cathedral town called Cloisterham in *The Mystery of Edwin Drood*.

One of the novel's key characters, John Jasper, is choirmaster at the cathedral. But as the novel reveals in its opening pages, he's also an opium smoker who travels to London to get his fix in an East End drug den. Jasper, it appears, is a conflicted man, subject to impulses he can't control.

Jasper's nephew and ward, the fatherless Edwin Drood, is a self-described "surface kind of fellow" who—when the novel opens—is engaged to a "blooming schoolgirl," Rosa Bud. Drood isn't quite certain he wants to marry Rosa. Jasper, however, wants her greatly. He hints of his longing—of stray aspirations left unfulfilled. And then Edwin Drood disappears...

Dickens designed *Drood* to appear in twelve monthly numbers: he finished six before he died. Over the years, many readers and critics have approached the novel as if it were, in fact, a mystery novel in which Dickens would plant clues until the killer of Edwin Drood was at last disclosed. Jasper, to be sure, is the leading suspect. But what of Neville Landless, who is like a gypsy, we're told, and "untamed," and who quarreled with Drood? And who is Dick Datchery, the curious lodger with white hair and black eyebrows?

Dickens' readers were hooked, and sales of the serial reached fifty thousand copies. "It has very, very far outstripped every one of its predecessors," Dickens noted happily in one of his letters.

Dickens had of course dealt with crime and mystery before. But *The Mystery of Edwin Drood* allowed him to lean more explicitly in the direction of "sensation fiction" that was coming into vogue. Dickens himself had helped define the genre with such works as *Bleak House* and *Great Expectations*. Such works, including *The Moonstone* and Mary Braddon's *Lady Audley's Secret* (1862), drew artfully on the conventions of popular melodrama while adding on pronounced elements of mystery and crime. Think bats, ravens, shadows, looming scandals, skulking foreigners and foggy churchyards.

Edmund Wilson took interest in Dickens' long interest in the criminal mind. Bradley Headstone in *Our Mutual Friend* is, Wilson suggests, particularly intriguing. He's a head case for sure: "perverted, tormented, confused," as Wilson writes—a young schoolteacher full of keen desires and gnawing insecurities. He's desperate to marry Lizzie Hexam, and he's "wounded by her preference for Eugene Wrayburn, whose nonchalance and grace infuriate him because he knows he can never achieve them." When his rage and lust finally overwhelm him, writes Wilson, Bradley becomes more frightening than such figures as Bill Sikes or Jonas Chuzzlewit because "we understand Bradley as a human being. Bradley is the first murderer in Dickens who exhibits any complexity of character."

Or, as Headstone himself declares when confronting Lizzie: "No man knows till the time comes what depths are within him. To some men it never comes; let them rest and be thankful! To me, you brought it; on me, you forced it; and the bottom of this raging sea, striking himself upon the breast, has been heaved up ever since."

John Jasper is constructed in much the same vein. He is not an obvious grotesque, but a presumably respectable man. Dickens suggests he is double-sided, and skilled in certain esoteric arts. He may be a skilled mesmerist, like Dickens himself. He's certainly focused his animal magnetism on Rosa Bud. Jasper gives Rosa music lessons. But he's also "made me a slave of me with his looks" as Rosa complains. "He has forced me to understand him, without his saying a word; and he has forced me to keep silence, without his uttering a threat. When I play, he never moves his eyes from my hands. When I sing, he never moves his eyes from my lips. When he corrects me, and strikes a note, or a chord, or plays a passage, he himself is in the sounds, whispering that he pursues me as a lover, and commanding me to keep his secret."

Wilson was among the first to suggest that John Jasper was a Thug, or in some way linked to the "Indian sect of Thugs, who made a profession of ingratiating themselves with travelers and then strangling them with a handkerchief and robbing them."

The Thugs fascinated Dickens' contemporaries, and were featured in several bestselling books like Meadows Tyler's *Confessions of a Thug* (1839), much admired by England's young queen. Victoria and many of her subjects were much enthralled by the whole mystique that surrounded the Thugs, not least the way they adapted clever disguises and were highly adept at concealing all proof of their crimes. The Thugs were respected members of their villages or communities. But they were also members of a secret society linked to the practice of human sacrifice and the worship of the Hindu goddess Kali.

As Wilson notes, Wilkie Collins'

1870

1868 novel *The Moonstone* had also included "a band of Hindu devotees" who carry out a secret murder in England. And Dickens' friend, the novelist Edward Bulwer-Lytton, had also considered using a Thug-linked storyline. For Dickens, however, the whole notion of these figures with split-personalities held a special appeal. As Wilson suggests, he'd become such a man himself—the widely hailed novelist and champion of Christmas cheer who had broken up his own large household in order to live, with an actress, his own secret life.

As Wilson also notes, Dickens' final novels appear at the same time he was presenting, in his literary readings, Sikes' murder of Nancy in *Oliver Twist*. Dickens read the scene with brio, even though—as Wilson notes—a "woman's doctor of his acquaintance" had warned him that "if only one woman cries out when you murder the girl, there will be a contagion of hysteria all over the place." But Dickens "obviously derived from thus horrifying his hearers some sort of satisfaction." And in fact his imagination "had always been subject to a tendency of this kind." Like the Fat Boy in the *Pickwick Papers*, Dickens quite enjoyed making your flesh creep. Some parts of Dickens' work remind us of Charlie Chaplin. Other parts recall Edgar Allen Poe.

But was *The Mystery of Edwin Drood* meant to be, in fact, a mystery—a great forerunner of *Who Killed Roger Ackroyd?* and countless similar titles? Over the years many writers—including Charles Forsyte, Leon Garfield and Carlo Fruttero and Franco Lucentini—have offered complete versions of the story after studying its characters and sorting its clues. In the 1980s, Rupert Holmes' popular musical version of the novel invited the audience to help solve the question: *Who Killed Edwin Drood?*

John Forster, however, had revealed Dickens' intentions long ago. Forster wrote that Jasper had, in fact, killed Edwin. Moreover, Dickens planned to have Jasper assume the book's narration. He would admit to the crime from the prison cell where he sat condemned. And Rosa would marry Liutenant R.N. Tartar, not a brooding, self-absorbed music master, but a robust, broad-shouldered man with a sunburned face.

Charles Dickens

A WALK IN A WORKHOUSE.

Household Words, Vol. 1, No. 9,   *May 25, 1850.*

On a certain Sunday, I formed one of the congregation assembled in the chapel of a large metropolitan Workhouse. With the exception of the clergyman and clerk, and a very few officials, there were none but paupers present. The children sat in the galleries; the women in the body of the chapel, and in one of the side aisles; the men in the remaining aisle. The service was decorously performed, though the sermon might have been much better adapted to the comprehension and to the circumstances of the hearers. The usual supplications were offered, with more than the usual significancy in such a place, for the fatherless children and widows, for all sick persons and young children, for all that were desolate and oppressed, for the comforting and helping of the weak-hearted for the raising up of them that had fallen; for all that were in danger, necessity, and tribulation. The prayers of the congregation were desired "for several persons in the various wards dangerously ill;" and others who were recovering returned their thanks to Heaven.

Among this congregation, were some evil-looking young women, and beetle-browed young men; but not many—perhaps that kind of characters kept away. Generally, the faces (those of the children excepted) were depressed and subdued, and wanted colour. Aged people were there, in every variety. Mumbling, blear-eyed, spectacled, stu-pid, deaf, lame; vacantly winking in the gleams of sun that now and then crept in through the open doors, from the paved yard; shading their listening ears, or blinking eyes, with their withered hands; poring over their books, leering at nothing, going to sleep, crouching and drooping in corners. There were weird old women, all skeleton within, all bonnet and cloak without, continually wiping their eyes with dirty dusters of pocket-handker chiefs; and there were ugly old crones, both male and female, with a ghastly kind of contentment upon them which was not at all comforting to see. Upon the whole, it was the dragon, Pauperism, in a very weak and impotent condition; toothless, fangless, drawing his breath heavily enough, and hardly worth chaining up.

When the service was over, I walked with the humane and conscientious gentleman whose duty it was to take that walk, that Sunday morning, through the little world of poverty enclosed within the workhouse walls. It was inhabited by a population of some fifteen hundred or two thousand paupers, ranging from the infant newly born or not yet come into the pauper world, to the old man dying on his bed.

In a room opening from a squalid yard, where a number of listless women were lounging to and fro, trying to get warm in the ineffectual sunshine of the tardy May morning—in the "Itch Ward," not to compromise the truth—

Household Words, Vol. 1, No. 9,   *May 25, 1850.*

a woman such as Hocauru has often drawn, was hurriedly getting on her gown before a dusty fire. She was the nurse, or wardswoman, of that insalubrious department—herself a pauper—flabby, raw-boned, untidy—unpromising and coarse of aspect as need be. But, on being spoken to about the patients whom she had in charge, she turned round, with her shabby gown half on, half off, and fell a crying with all her might. Not for show, not querulously, not in any mawkish sentiment, but in the deep grief and affliction of her heart; turning away her dishevelled head: sobbing most bitterly, wringing her hands, and letting fall abundance of great tears, that choked her utterance. What was the matter with the nurse of the itch-ward? Oh, "the dropped child" was dead? Oh, the child that was found in the street, and she had brought up ever since, had died an hour ago, and see where the little creature lay, beneath this cloth! The dear, the pretty dear!

The dropped child seemed too small and poor a thing for Death to be in earnest with, but Death had taken it; and already its diminutive form was neatly washed, composed, and stretched as if in sleep upon a box. I thought I heard a voice from Heaven saying, It shall be well for thee, O nurse of the itch-ward, when some less gentle pauper does those offices to thy cold form, that such as the dropped child are the angels who behold my Father's face!

In another room, were several ugly old women crouching, witch like, round a hearth, and chattering and nodding, after the manner of the monkeys. "All well here? And enough to eat?" A general chattering and chuckling; at last an answer from a volunteer. "Oh yes gentleman I

Bless you gentleman! Lord bless the Parish of St. So-and-So! It feed the hungry, sir, and give drink to the thusty, and it warm them which is cold, so it do, and good luck to the parish of St. So-and-So, and thankee gentleman!" Elsewhere, a party of pauper nurses were at dinner. "How do you get on?" "Oh pretty well, sir! We works hard, and we lives hard—like the sodgers!"

In another room, a kind of purgatory or place of transition, six or eight noisy mad-women were gathered together, under the superintendence of one sane attendant. Among them was a girl of two or three-and-twenty, very prettily dressed, of most respectable appearance, and good manners, who had been brought in from the house where she had lived as domestic servant (having, I suppose, no friends), on account of being subject to epileptic fits, and requiring to be removed under the influence of a very bad one. She was by no means of the same stuff, or the same breeding, or the same experience, or in the same state of mind, as those by whom she was surrounded; and she pathetically complained that the daily association and the nightly noise made, her worse, and was driving her mad—which was perfectly evident. The case was noted for inquiry and redress, but she said she had already been there for some weeks.

If this girl had stolen her mistress's watch, I do not hesitate to say she would have been infinitely better off. We have come to this absurd, this dangerous, this monstrous pass, that the dishonest felon is, in respect of cleanliness, order, diet, and accommodation, better provided for, and taken care of, than the honest pauper.

And this conveys no special imputation on the workhouse of the parish of St. So-

Household Words, Vol. 1, No. 9,   *May 25, 1850.*

-and-So, where, on the contrary, I saw many things to commend. It was very agreeable, recollecting that most infamous and atrocious enormity committed at Tooting—an enormity which, a hundred years hence, will still be vividly remembered in the bye-ways of English life, and which has done more to engender a gloomy discontent and suspicion among many thousands of the people than all the Chartist leaders could have done in all their lives—to find the pauper children in this workhouse looking robust and well and apparently the objects of very great care. In the Infant School—a large, light, airy room at the top of the building—the little creatures, being at dinner, and eating their potatoes heartily, were not cowed by the presence of strange visitors, but stretched out their small hands to be shaken, with a very pleasant confidence. And it was comfortable to see two mangey pauper rocking-horses rampant in a corner. In the girls' school, where the dinner was also in progress, everything bore a cheerful and healthy aspect. The meal was over, in the boys' school, by the time of our arrival there, and the room was not yet quite rearranged; but the boys were roaming unrestrained about a large and airy yard, as any other schoolboys might have done. Some of them had been drawing large ships upon the schoolroom wall; and if they bad a mast with shrouds and stays set up for practice (as they have in the Middlesex House of Correction), it would be so much the better. At present, if a boy should feel a strong impulse upon him to learn the art of going aloft, he could only gratify it, I presume, as the men and women paupers gratify their as-

pirations after better board and lodging, by smashing as many workhouse windows as possible, and being promoted to prison.

In one place, the Newgate of the Workhouse, a company of boys and youths were locked up in a yard alone; their day-room being a kind of kennel where the casual poor used formerly to be littered down at night. Divers of them had been there some long time. "Are they never going away "was the natural inquiry. "Most of them are crippled, in some form or other," said "the Wardsman,"and not fit for anything." They slunk about, like dispirited wolves or hyaenas; and made a pounce at their food when it was served out, much as those animals do. The big-headed idiot shuffling his feet along the pavement, in the sunlight outside, was a more agreeable object in everyway.

Groves of babies in arms; groves of mothers and other sick women in bed; groves of lunatics; jungles of men in stone-paved down-stairs day-rooms, waiting for their dinners; longer and longer groves of old people, in upstairs Infirmary wards, wearing out life, God knows how—this was the scenery through which the walk lay, for two hours. In some of these latter chambers, there were pictures stuck against the wall, and a neat display of crockery and pewter on a kind of sideboard; now and then it was a treat to see a plant or two; in almost every ward there was a cat.

In all of these Long Walks of aged and infirm, some old people were bedridden, and had been for a long time; some were sitting on their beds half-naked; some dying in their beds; some of no use, dogged

Household Words, Vol. 1, No. 9,   *May 25, 1850.*

and being out of bed, and sitting at a table near the fire. A sullen or lethargic indifference to what was asked, a blunted sensibility to everything but warmth and food, a moody absence of complaint as being of no use, a dogged silence and resentful desire to be left alone again, I thought were generally apparent. On our walking into the midst of one of these dreary perspectives of old men, nearly the following little dialogue took place, the nurse not being immediately at hand:

"All well here?"

No answer. An old man in a Scotch cap sitting among others on a form at the table, eating out of a tin porringer, pushes back his cap a little to look at us, claps it down on his forehead again with the palm of his hand, and goes on eating.

"All well here?" (repeated.)

No answer. Another old man sitting on his bed, paralytically peeling a boiled potato, lifts his head and stares.

"Enough to eat?"

No answer. Another old man, in bed, turns himself and coughs.

"How are you today?" To the last old man.

That old man says nothing; but another old man, a tall old man of very good address, speaking with perfect correctness, comes forward from somewhere, and volunteers an answer. The reply almost always proceeds from a volunteer, and not from the person looked at or spoken to.

"We are very old, sir," in a mild, distinct voice. "We can't expect to be well, most of us."

"Are you comfortable?"

"I have no complaint to make, sir."

With a half shake of his head, a half shrug of his shoulders, and a kind of apologetic smile.

"Enough to eat!"

"Why, sir, I have but a poor appetite," with the same air as before; "and yet I get through my allowance very easy."

"But," showing a porringer with a Sunday dinner in it; "here is a portion of mutton, and three potatoes. You can't starve on that?"

"Oh dear no, sir," with the same apologetic air. "Not starve."

"What do you want?"

"We have very little bread, sir. It's an exceedingly small quantity of bread."

The nurse, who is now rubbing her hands at the questioner's elbow, interferes with, "It ain't much raly, sir. You see they've only six ounces a day, and when they've took their breakfast, there can only be a little left for night, sir."

Another old man, hitherto invisible, rises out of his bed-clothes, as out of a grave, and looks on.

"You have tea at night?" The questioner is still addressing the well-spoken old man.

"Yes, sir, we have tea at night."

"And you save what bread you can from the morning, to eat with it"

"Yes, sir—if we can save any."

"And you want more to eat with it?"

"Yes, sir." With a very anxious face.

The questioner, in the kindness of his heart, appears a little discomposed, and changes the subject.

"What has become of the old man who used to lie in that bed in the corner?"

The nurse don't remember what old man is referred to. There has been such a many old men. The well-spoken

Household Words, Vol. 1, No. 9,   *May 25, 1850.*

old man is doubtful. The spectral old man who has come to life in bed, says, "Billy Stevens." Another old man who has previously had his head in the fireplace, pipes out:

"Charley Walters."

Something like a feeble interest is awakened. I suppose Charley Walters had conversation in him.

"He's dead," says the piping old man.

Another old man, with one eye screwed up, hastily displaces the piping old man, and says:

"Yes! Charley Walters died in that bed, and — and —" "Billy Stevens," persists the spectral old man.

"No, no! and Johnny Rogers died in that bed, and—they're both on 'em dead—and Sarn'l Bowyer;" this seems very extraordinary to him; "he went out!"

With this he subsides, and all the old men (having had quite enough of it) subside, and the spectral old man goes into his grave again, and takes the shade of Billy Stevens with him.

As we turn to go out at the door, another previously invisible old man, a hoarse old man in a flannel gown, is standing there, as if he had just come up through the floor.

"I beg your pardon, sir, could I take the liberty of saying a word?"

"Yes; what is it?"

"I am greatly better in my health, sir; but what I want, to get me quite round," with his hand on his throat, "is a little fresh air, sir. It has always done my complaint so much good, sir. The regular leave for going out, comes round so seldom, that if the gentlemen, next Friday, would give me leave to go out walking, now and then— for only an hour or so, sir! —"

Who could wonder, looking through those weary vistas of bed and infirmity, that it should do him good to meet with some other scenes, and assure himself that there was something else on earth? Who could help wondering why the old men lived on as they did; what grasp they had on life; what crumbs of interest or occupation they could pick up from its bare board; whether Charley Walters had ever described to them the days when he kept company with some old pauper woman in the bud, or Billy Stevens ever told them of the time when he was a dweller in the far-off foreign land called Home!

The morsel of burnt child, lying in another room, so patiently, in bed, wrapped in lint, and looking steadfastly at us with his bright quiet eyes when we spoke to him kindly, looked as if the knowledge of these things, and of all the tender things there are to think about, might have been in his mind—as if he thought, with us, that there was a fellow-feeling in the pauper nurses which appeared to make them more kind to their charges than the race of common nurses in the hospitals —as if he mused upon the Future of some older children lying around him in the same place, and thought it best, perhaps, all things considered, that he should die—as if he knew, without fear, of those many coffins, made and unmade, piled up in the store below—and of his unknown friend, "the dropped child," calm upon the box-lid covered with a cloth. But there was something wistful and appealing, too, in his tiny face, as if, in the midst of all the hard necessities and incongruities he pondered on, he pleaded, in behalf of the helpless and the aged poor, for a little more liberty—and a little more bread.

Dean Arthur Stanley on Dickens

❝ He whom we mourn was the friend of mankind, a philanthropist in the true sense; the friend of youth, the friend of the poor, the enemy of every form of meanness and oppression. I am not going to attempt to draw a portrait of him. Men of genius are different from what we suppose them to be. They have greater pleasures and greater pains, greater affections and greater temptations, than the generality of mankind, and they can never be altogether understood by their fellow-men.... But we feel that a light has gone out, that the world is darker to us, when they depart. There are so very few of them that we cannot afford to lose them one by one, and we look vainly round for others who may supply their places. He whose loss we now mourn occupied a greater space than any other writer in the minds of Englishmen during the last thirty-three years. We read him, talked about him, acted him; we laughed with him; we were roused by him to a consciousness of the misery of others, and to a pathetic interest in human life. Works of fiction, indirectly, are great instructors of this world; and we can hardly exaggerate the debt of gratitude which is due to a writer who has led us to sympathise with these good, true, sincere, honest English characters of ordinary life, and to laugh at the egotism, the hypocrisy, the false respectability of religious professors and others. To another great humorist who lies in this church the words have been applied that his death eclipsed the gaiety of nations. But of him who has been recently taken I would rather say, in humbler language, that no one was ever so much beloved or so much mourned. ❞

—**June, 1870**

Sources and Credits

....

The world is full of good books and essays about Charles Dickens. For this study I benefitted particularly from: John Forster's *The Life of Charles Dickens* (1874); G.K. Chesterton, *Charles Dickens* (1906); Malcolm Elwin, *Victorian Wallflowers: A Panoramic Survey of the Popular Literary Periodicals* (1934); George Orwell, "Charles Dickens," *Inside the Whale* (1940); Edmund Wilson, "Dickens: The Two Scrooges," *The Wound and the Bow* (1941); Walter Allen, *Six Great Novelists* (1955); Earle R. Davis, *The Flint and the Flame: The Artistry of Charles Dickens* (1963); Edward Wagenknecht, *Dickens and the Scandalmongers* (1965); Michael Goldebrg, *Carlyle and Dickens* (1972); John Carey, *The*

Violent Effigy (1973); Anne Lohrli, *Household Words: A Weekly Journal Conducted by Charles Dickens* (1973); Alfred Harbage, *A Kind of Power: The Shakespeare-Dickens Analogy* (1975); Michael Slater, ed. *Dickens on America and the Americans* (1978); Harry Stone, *Dickens and the Invisible World* (1980); Sidney Moss, *Charles Dickens' Quarrel with America* (1984); Myron Magnet, *Dickens and the Social Order* (1984); Michael Pointer, *Charles Dickens on the Screen* (1996); Fred Guida, *A Christmas Carol and Its Adaptations* (1999); John Glavin, *Dickens on Screen* (2003); David Parker, *Christmas and Charles Dickens* (2005); John Walker, *The Real Oliver Twist: Robert Blincoe, a Life that Illustrates a Violent Age* (2007); John Sutherland: *How to Read a Novel: A User's Guide* (2007).

Also, among memoirs, biographies, and historical studies: George Sala, *Charles Dickens: An Essay* (1870); W.T. Price, *A Life of William Charles Macready* (1890); Mamie Dickens, *My Father as I Recall Him* (1897); Percy Fitzgerald, *Memories of Charles Dickens* (1913); J. W.T. Ley, *The Dickens Circle: A Narrative of the Novelist's Friendships* (1919); Oliver Elton, *Dickens and Thackeray* (1924); Henry F. Dickens, *Memories of My Father* (1928); Gladys Storey, *Dickens and Daughter* (1939); Jack Lindsay, *Charles Dickens* (1950); Edgar Johnson, *Charles Dickens: His Tragedy and Triumph* (1952); J. B. Priestly, *Charles Dickens and his World* (1961); Wolf Mankowitz,, *Dickens of London* (1976); Norman and Jean Mackenzie, *Dickens: A Life* (1979); Diana Orton, *Made of Gold: A Biography of Angela Burdett Coutts* (1980);Fred Kaplan, *Dickens: A Biography* (1988); Claire Tomalin, *The Invisible Woman: The Story of Nelly Ternan and Charles Dickens* (1990); Peter Ackroyd, *Dickens* (1990); D. J. Taylor, *Thackeray* (1999); Alison Winter, *Mesmerized: Powers of Mind in Victorian Britain* (2000); A. N. Wilson *The Victorians* (2004); Lucinda Hawksley, *Katey: The Life and Loves of Dickens' Artist Daughter* (2006); Ben Wilson, *The Making of Victorian Values: Decency and Dissent in Britain 1789-1837* (2007).

These collections are also invaluable: *The Letters of Charles Dickens, 12 vols., The Pilgrim Edition* (1965-2003), and Michael Slater, ed. *The Dent Uniform Edition of Dickens' Journalism* (4 volumes, 1994-2000). Catherine Dickens' recipes and menues are found in *Dinner for Dickens: The Culinary History of Mrs. Charles Dickens's Menu Books,* by Susan Rossi-Wilcox (2005).

Illustrations

Cover photograph courtesy of **Dickens House Museum**, London; London street children, **Dickens House Museum**; Ellen Ternan (p.38) **Dickens House Museum**; Catherine Hogarth Dickens (p.40), courtesy of **Dickens House Museum**. Original drawings by **Darren Gygi** (pgs. 64, 122, 138). Cast of *Pickwick Papers* (p.142); **Dickens House Museum**; Bernard Hepton (p.113) and Colin Hurley (p.143) from **Mobil MasterpieceTheatre** production of *David Copperfield* (1986). Additional graphics (pgs. 31, 59, 120, 131) from the **U. S. Library of Congress** archive.

Other cartoons and illustrations are drawn principally from books by Dickens' friends or contemporaries, including Mark Lemon, *Up and Down the London Streets* (1886), George Sala's *America Revisited: From the Bay of New York to the Gulf of Mexico and From Lake Michigan to the Pacific* (1882), Sala's *Living London; or, Echoes Re-echoed* (1883), Joseph Hatton, *Journalistic London: Famous Pens and Papers of the Day* (1882); Chauncey Hare Townshend, *Facts in Mesmerism* (1841); as well as from Henry Mayhew's *London Labour and London Poor* (London: William Kimber, 1954).

The drawings of George Cruikshank, one of Dickens' earliest illustrators, are also found throughout the book (pgs. 33, 52, 76, 84, 133) and in his *Four Hundred Humorous Illustrations* (*n. d.*).

Acknowledgments

Cover design by Julia Evins at Evins Design, Baltimore, Maryland. Book design by Diana Samet. For production help and research assistance I am also grateful to John McIntyre, Jennifer Ladd, Peggy Feild, and the Dickens House Museum. Also, thanks to Document Services at Loyola College and Digital Access Services at the Loyola Notre Dame Library.